SALONS
The Joy of Conversation

SALONS

The Joy of Conversation

JAIDA N'HA SANDRA
JON SPAYDE

AND THE EDITORS OF UTNE READER

AN *UTNE READER* BOOK

NEW SOCIETY PUBLISHERS

Cataloguing in Publication Data: A catalog record for this publication is available from the National Library of Canada.

Cover design by Richard Aquan. Cover image by Gary Kelley.

Printed in Canada by Friesens Inc.

New Society Publishers acknowledges the support of the Government of Canada through the Book Publishing Industry Development Program (BPIDP) for our publishing activities, and the assistance of the Province of British Columbia through the British Columbia Arts Council.

BRITISH
COLUMBIA
ARTS COUNCIL
Supported by the Province of British Columbia

Paperback ISBN: 0-86571-444-4

Inquiries regarding requests to reprint all or part of *Salons: The Joy of Conversation* should be addressed to New Society Publishers at the address below.

To order directly from the publishers, please add $4.50 shipping to the price of the first copy, and $1.00 for each additional copy (plus GST in Canada). Send check or money order to:

New Society Publishers
P.O. Box 189, Gabriola Island, BC V0R 1X0, Canada

Published in cooperation with *Utne Reader* Books, 1624, Harmon Place, Minneapolis, MN 55403 www.utne.com

New Society Publishers' mission is to publish books that contribute in fundamental ways to building an ecologically sustainable and just society, and to do so with the least possible impact on the environment, in a manner that models this vision. We are committed to doing this not just through education, but through action. We are acting on our commitment to the world's remaining ancient forests by phasing out our paper supply from ancient forests worldwide. This book is one step towards ending global deforestation and climate change. It is printed on acid-free paper that is **100% old growth forest-free** (100% post-consumer recycled), processed chlorine free, and printed with vegetable based, low VOC inks. For further information, or to browse our full list of books and purchase securely, visit our website at: www.newsociety.com

NEW SOCIETY PUBLISHERS   **www.newsociety.com**

CONTENTS

PART ONE ≈ History: A Tradition of Talk

PART TWO ≈ Foundations: Getting Your Salon Started

PART THREE ≈ Big Talk: The Art of Salon Conversation

PART FOUR ≈ Variations on a Theme: Other Salon Directions

APPENDIX

A Minneapolis coffeehouse is filled with diffuse midmorning sunlight. Tapestries and colorful paintings hang on the walls. The aroma of coffee and muffins wafts through the air. Some twenty media junkies stir in a loose circle of well-worn, comfortable old chairs, each of a different design. A three-hour discussion is launched with this question: "What have you been thinking and obsessing about lately?" Thus begins the *Utne Reader* Salon.

Salons are the most stimulating aspect of producing *Utne Reader*. When the coffee is strong and the chemistry is right, our conversations seem to tap directly into the zeitgeist. One person's ideas inspire another's and another's. Each contributes a piece of something larger. By making explicit what may have been, prior to the salon, only flickering at the edges of our awareness, these heady gab sessions turn into something transcendent—conversational and conceptual jazz.

In the March/April 1991 issue of *Utne Reader*, we published a cover section called "Salons: How to Revive the Endangered Art of Conversation and Start a Revolution in Your Neighborhood." Since then, the salon phenomenon has turned into a movement. Thousands of book clubs, church circles, office work groups, and even dinner parties, inspired by the *Utne Reader* articles, have transformed themselves into salons or salon permutations: councils (more meditative, with the emphasis on listening and speaking from the heart) or study circles (more intensive and goal-oriented).

Our distant ancestors gathered around the fire. Since then, most cultures have had some social form like the salon. It's just basic to being human—people need to get together and talk over the things they care about and believe in. In the United States, television and the accelerated pace of modern life seem to be the principal forces that undermine conversational gatherings. The current resurgence of salons may herald a turning point in American history. As more and more people turn off the tube and reach out to each other, direct, person-to-person, community-based democracy can begin to flourish once again.

Indeed, salons could be the antidote for the sense of alienation and malaise that currently infects much of America. They're fun. They're glamorous and evocative of eighteenth-century Paris. And yet they're as simple to produce as a coffee klatch. I believe they might even change the world. Are you up for a cultural revolution?

~ Eric Utne

ACKNOWLEDGMENTS

Thanks to all those salon members who have shared their homes and memories with me. Although I can't list them all, I am particularly indebted to Avaren Ipsen and Victoria Woolley of the Lowry Hill Salon, Judith Bell of the Loring Neighborhood Salon, both in Minneapolis, and all my friends at the Berkeley Creativity Salon. Steven Grover and Alan Lipton, thank you for keeping the salon alive while I went off to write this book. My love also to my housemates at the Tree House.

Special thanks to John and Lori, owners of the wonderful Coffee Gallery in Minneapolis. Susan Burr, thank you for insights and information on the meetings of the Friends. My optometrist, Herb Monroe, has always helped me see my way more clearly, figuratively as well as literally. My gratitude also to the *Utne Reader* staff for generously answering questions and sharing resources. Jules Inda, Carolyn Adams, Griff Wigley, Patti Cich, and Elizabeth Larsen all provided enormous support. Above all, thank you, Eric Utne, for seeing my potential and taking a gamble on an unknown author.

Finally, this book is dedicated to my two fathers: Gary Bethke, who welcomed me home when I seemed farthest from home, and Leslie Gerber, who has unfailingly believed in my ability to realize any dream. I love you both.

~ Jaida n'ha Sandra

The revision of *The Joy of Conversation* couldn't have happened without the willingness of Patti Cich and Terrence Gotz to give of their knowledge, time, and energy. Julie Ristau made the impossible possible and even enjoyable. Love to my old buddy Max Carmichael, a true visionary who showed me what human synergy is all about, and to the whole Minneapolis Tertulia gang at Tracy's Saloon: Joe Hart, Brian Felland, Maria Fitzgerald, Robert Fitzgerald, Christine Capra, Hari Capra, both Mark Andersons, Carolyn Crooke, Kristina Sigler, Maureen Aitken, Matt Helling, and drop-in guests over the years. Their energy and unflagging sense of fun turned my simple salon idea into a wonderful ongoing experiment.

Finally, a tip of the hat and much thanks to my former *Utne* colleague Joshua Glenn, for updating and adding his expertise to the chapter on online salons. Founder-editor of *Hermenaut*, America's hippest and funniest journal of philosophy and cultural theory, Josh is living proof that lively minds can do serious intellectual work outside of academia. Come to think of it, the whole salon movement is living proof of the very same point.

~ Jon Spayde

INTRODUCTION

To converse is human. To salon is divine.

Salons are gatherings where people talk big talk, talk meant to be listened to and perhaps passionately acted upon. Salons are incubators where ideas are conceived, gestated, and hatched, sometimes slowly and ruminatively, sometimes with dazzling speed. Salons are the frontiers of social and cultural change. Salons are the concert halls where conversation is presented in virtuoso style. They've been flourishing since ancient Greece, and they're going on in America right now. Anyone can start one; all it takes is willingness.

The authors of this book are two cases in point. Jaida n'ha Sandra founded the Creativity Salon in Berkeley, California, in 1990 in an effort to connect with a community. Jaida had spent several years in Japan, where she was impressed by the family and community support each individual seemed to receive. Her return to the United States brought with it a shocking awareness of isolation. "I decided not to travel again until I had carved out a home in my own culture," she says. "The Creativity Salon was part of this effort. It was a way of reaching out to a wider circle of acquaintances and building, over time, a community of memory. The other, at first more important, reason for starting a salon was to practice creativity in a setting where I needn't fear judgment of my efforts. The salon was an experiment in approaching art playfully. By starting a group where criticism was not allowed, I hoped to subdue my internal critic."

A year later, the regular members of the salon told her that it had become a touchstone in their lives. Within two years, more than seventy people were on the list of interested participants. "I had come to know a more diverse group of people," says Jaida. "I had a wider circle of supportive and trustworthy friends than ever before. I became able to take greater and greater creative risks. And, for the first time, I believed in my ability to have an impact on other people's lives and the larger society. The salon was a success."

In the early 1980s, Jon Spayde (with his close friend Max Carmichael) organized evenings of performance and conversation in Max's San Francisco loft. These evenings featured live Moroccan music and punk rock, dramatic readings, fire juggling (soon brought to a halt by the police), and intense talk. Looking for a way to make the evenings both bigger and more focused, Max organized his legendary Pow-Wows—freestyle gatherings in the loft (and later in the California desert) where artists, tech-heads, educational visionaries, painters, and neo-country-western singers ate, sang, danced, talked, and inspired one another.

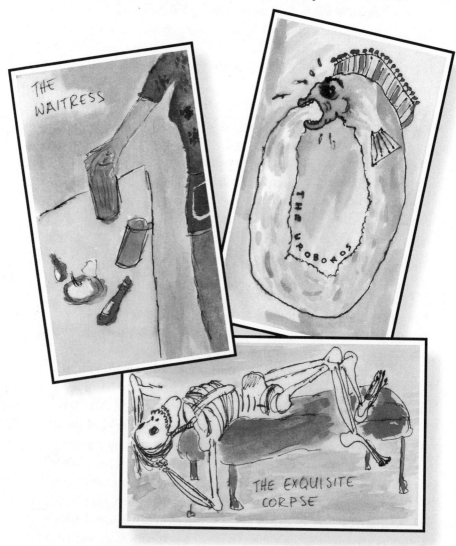

Handmade Tarot cards from the Tracy's Tertulia, Minneapolis

A decade later, Jon organized the Tertulia, a free-form saloon-based salon in Minneapolis that's still going strong after eight years. Originally conceived as a gathering of fiction writers and poets, the Tertulia is not a standard writers' group. Instead of critiquing one another's work, the Tertulians go in for activities that reflect the Group Mind: surrealist "exquisite corpse" collaborative writing, complex conversational riffs that delve into conspiracy scenarios involving Jesse Ventura and Prince, and even the development of a brand-new Tarot deck based on the members' experiences and obsessions—which they use for uncannily precise readings of the future.

Salons are not necessarily set up to achieve goals. This fact makes some Americans a little uneasy. We tend to want to commit to activities that make us stronger, smarter, more beautiful, richer; or, if we're idealists, to concrete plans that will make the world less hungry, less poor, and less barren. The salon makes no such promises. But the absence of specific goals does not mean that salons serve no purpose.

Several years ago, Jaida talked with a Tibetan Buddhist monk about the life of Tibetan refugees in Nepal. When the subject turned to education, he asserted that the Nepalese were, on the whole, better educated than Americans. Because at that time only 19 percent of the adults in Nepal could read, Jaida was taken aback. When she asked the monk to explain, he said that the Nepalese got more of an education because they discussed world events. "If only one person [in a family or village] can read," he said, "everyone knows what that person knows. The Nepalese talk about everything a lot, in restaurants, on buses. Everybody gets together and passes information to each other."

Salons are not necessarily set up to achieve goals. This fact makes some Americans a little uneasy.

In the monk's experience, Americans seemed to know little about anything except their jobs, and they rarely talked to anyone about matters of consequence. Yet anybody now living in the United States who reads or owns a television, radio, or computer encounters more information than has been available at any other time in history. But we risk ignorance because we tend to receive information passively, relying more on experts than on our own life experiences to make sense of what we take in. And the sheer volume of "input" means that no one can catch up with it completely, much less put the pieces together.

As the Tibetan monk implied, talking with others is a way out of this bind. Salons move beyond statistics and facts toward genuine understanding. They encourage us to probe the complexities of our world. In salons, we have the chance to talk over the things we are privately concerned about, to grasp the views of those who have had experiences different from our own, and to arrive at some understanding of where we can go from here. In salons, people search for meaning and come to trust their own ability to evaluate the information that is thrown at them. The most exciting salon experience is finding yourself saying something with conviction that you hadn't previously realized you knew or believed. In the moment of speaking, you discover your own wisdom.

Salon conversations also bring people together. Salonists gain the skills of democratic participation. They learn how to organize a group and keep it running. They practice abandoning no-win dichotomies and finding consensus. They gain the confidence to interact with the larger world, drawing on their fellow salonists for support.

Important changes don't often occur as a result of sudden, earth-shattering events. They happen in increments, through a slow buildup of fragile, almost imperceptible experiences. Gradual alterations in attitudes and opinions add up, until you find yourself doing something you know you wouldn't have done a year ago, five years ago, a decade ago. Salons are communities where such tiny alterations occur and evolve into something meaningful.

Because there is no one best way to conduct a salon, this book attempts to be descriptive rather than prescriptive. And, most of all, it attempts to inspire. We want to invite you to join the great and glamorous salon tradition in your own way. And show you how classic salon-keepers like Julie de Lespinasse, Mabel Dodge, and Gertrude Stein fostered, furthered, and flavored the art of conversation, and what you can learn from them in forming and enjoying your own salon.

PART ONE

HISTORY:

A TRADITION OF TALK

CHAPTER ONE

ORIGINS:
FROM ANCIENT GREECE
TO THE TWENTIETH CENTURY

The men and women of salons speak to us across centuries, encouraging us with their determination to educate and express themselves, inspiring us with their love of humanity and their compassion for human failings. The breadth, subtlety, and complexity of their thought and the intensity of their involvement in the world can still inspire us.

Salonists have always eagerly debated the fundamental philosophical ideas that were transforming their societies. They have grappled with questions of human rights and liberties; with conflicts between church, state, and science; with education, feminism, sexuality, law, and developments in the arts and sciences. Passionate conversation often led to passionate action, to lives risked and sometimes sacrificed in efforts to achieve social and political change. People who might elsewhere have been socially ostracized were included in salons—welcomed for their wit, intelligence, charm, and insight.

THE FIRST SALONS

The precursors of European salons were the symposia of ancient Greece. Symposia took place in private homes, in special rooms built for the purpose. These rooms, called *andron*, were present in every house, from those owned by the wealthiest Athenians to those of the poorest farmers. During gatherings in the *andron*, an intimate group of guests ate, drank, and discussed everything from local gossip to politics and philosophy. The guests sometimes were entertained by professional musicians or dancers, but more often they amused themselves by reciting poetry and passages from the dramatists, or by singing hymns, love songs, and drinking songs.

Egalitarian both in subject and in membership, the symposia brought together people from many occupations, from philosophers to farmers. This mix of people encouraged creative exchanges between followers of different disciplines and kept the more powerful members of society in healthy contact with ordinary citizens.

The ancient Romans imitated the symposia with elaborate and often decadent banquets. Again, people of all ranks dined together while discussing current events and showing off their talents. Banquets were so commonplace that they often escaped the scrutiny that suspicious Roman emperors directed at other gatherings.

The Roman habit of welcoming artists and writers into the homes of the elite continued throughout the centuries in Italy. Later, the French royalty became envious of Italian arts and scholarship. French kings returned from wars in Italy with writers and scholars in tow, determined to set up their own circles. Wealthy wives of merchants and royal women residing away from court began to imitate this new fad. The result was the birth of the French salon.

LITERARY CIRCLES OF THE SIXTEENTH CENTURY

The French salon came about when middle- and lower-ranking members of the nobility began to hold literary circles in their homes. These gatherings were often attended by scholars who hoped to win employment at court in any of several fields: writing poetry, teaching, practicing law, or working as private secretaries. They assembled in small groups based on common interests and ambitions.

> By the mid-1600s, a commoner who was sufficiently witty, worldly, and interesting might receive invitations to salons frequented by royalty.

Jean de Morel's home is one example of these gatherings. In 1541, Morel left Switzerland and took a position in Paris as a tutor. Two years later, he married Antoinette de Loynes, a well-educated young woman who shared many of her husband's intellectual interests. The couple welcomed into their home and advised unemployed poets, lawyers, and diplomats who had come to Paris seeking work. Jean de Morel used his influence with the author and patroness Princess Marguerite de France to gain pensions for his most talented friends. His house was praised as "le premier salon littéraire de Paris."

As the merchant class gained in wealth and power, class distinctions continued to erode. By the mid-1600s, a commoner who was sufficiently witty, worldly, and interesting might receive invitations to salons frequented by royalty. Soon, monied commoners began to hold their own literary circles, infringing on what had been an aristocratic prerogative.

This invasion didn't happen without a backlash: Some court circles were established specifically to exclude commoners. Noblemen who opposed social-mixing-by-conversation tended to regard salons as corrupt and an especially bad influence on women. They had reason to fear the influence of salon gatherings, for the egalitarianism of open conversation was emboldening members of all social classes. A democratic philosophy developed in these early salons that eventually would change the world.

MADAME DE RAMBOUILLET AND POLITE SOCIETY

Catharine de Rambouillet's Paris salon set the tone for seventeenth-century Europe. Repelled by the coarseness of palace life under Henry IV, Madame de Rambouillet retired to her own house, the Hôtel de Rambouillet, in 1607. Her salon, called by her guests the "sanctuary of the Temple of Athena," remained open until her death at the age of seventy-seven in 1665. By then she had established a standard of polite behavior, inspired countless women to set up their own salons, profoundly affected French literature, and established the foundation for a French social activity that would persist for two centuries.

Wealthy, beautiful, and of royal blood, Madame de Rambouillet was a stereotype of the classic salonkeeper. But her fortunate circumstances alone do not explain her great influence. More important were her strength of mind, her independence, and her desire to mold society into a form she found acceptable. She used her artistic skills to create a delightful and entertaining salon, welcoming to her home anyone she considered intellectually worthy and well-behaved.

This last criterion was strict. She flatly rejected those who did not meet her standards of politeness. Because she chose her guests wisely and expected them to behave virtuously, the opinions of the habitués of the Hôtel de Rambouillet came to be taken seriously by the rest of the world. The ambassador and writer Louis de Rouvroy Saint-Simon later described the group as a "tribunal with which it was necessary to count, and whose decisions upon the conduct and reputation of people of the court and the world had great weight."

The renowned Cardinal Richelieu so feared the salonists' opinions that he asked Madame de Rambouillet to pass along everything that was said in her salons. She diplomatically refused, pointing out that everyone knew of the friendship between them, so no one would dare speak badly of him. The tactfulness with which she turned aside intrigue with a compliment soon came to be emulated throughout the salons.

MADELEINE DE SCUDÉRY: AN EARLY FEMINIST

After Madame de Rambouillet's death, her friend Madeleine de Scudéry took over the Hôtel de Rambouillet. Initially, many factors counted against her by the standards of Parisian society: She had grown up in the countryside, had never married, and was considered exceptionally homely. Yet the salon she started at the age of sixty became famous. What "the Illustrious Sappho," as she was called, lacked in background, she made up for in education, thanks to an uncle who had encouraged

Madeleine de Scudéry

her in studies usually reserved for men (including Spanish and Italian, in which she became fluent). Her skill as a writer sparked a fashion in "pen portraits," highly complimentary essays on salon habitués. Her descriptions of salon dialogue reveal that she and her friends delighted in jokes and verbal play, especially puns.

Through the salon, Madeleine de Scudéry was able to express and find support for ideals that would later be considered feminist. She thought little of "light and coquettish women whose only occupation is to adorn their persons and pass their lives in fêtes and amusements—women who think that scrupulous virtue requires them to know nothing but to be the wife of a husband, the mother of children, and the mistress of the family; and men who regard women as upper servants, and forbid their daughters to read anything but prayer-books." The best kind of woman, she said, was one who "knows a hundred things of which she does not boast . . . has a well-informed mind, is familiar with fine works, speaks well, writes correctly, and knows the world."

De Scudéry was not alone in her views. The salons gave women a public voice and social influence. Salon women became increasingly well educated as their male guests suggested books for them to read and encouraged them to learn languages. Being leaders of salons gave women reason to imagine that they could become leaders in public life. Salon-keepers of the seventeenth century subverted gender norms simply by holding salons, but not until the eighteenth century did women move from admiring and inspiring men to realizing their own ambitions in the public sphere.

SALONS OF THE PHILOSOPHES

In the eighteenth century, salons were as numerous as women who had the time and resources to host them. There were hundreds throughout Paris and the provinces. Directories were published to assist foreign visitors who wanted to attend them. Through these conversational gatherings, women orchestrated the dissemination of radical theories, political rumors, and social gossip. They were able to make or break the political careers of men, and could insist on the airing of new ideas about human rights.

The most important movement supported by the eighteenth-century salons was the Enlightenment, the great rationalist, materialist, human-ist upsurge that directly threatened—and eventually transformed—both church and state. The Enlightenment was led by the philosophes—Voltaire, Jean-Jacques Rousseau, Jean Le Rond d'Alembert, Denis Diderot, and others—who propounded radical notions of liberty and equality, arguing for their beliefs in the ubiquitous salons. Although the philosophes were satirized, imprisoned, tortured, and exiled, their ideas spread, via the salons, into the general population. By the end of the cen-tury, those ideas would foster a complete social and political revolution.

Several salons served as rallying places for the philosophes. The same people frequented each of these salons, they all covered essentially the same topics, and each attempted to become the center of the new philosophy. Nevertheless, each salon was unique, thanks to the dis-tinctive characters of the salonkeepers.

One of the salons was run by a man—Baron d'Holbach, an eccentric misanthrope from Germany. An ardent materialist and atheist, d'Holbach devoted himself to the philosophes, introducing them to members of the aristocracy who might support their ideas. He also penned several hun-dred articles for their great project, the *Encyclopédie ou Dictionnaire Raisonné des Sciences, des Arts et des Métiers*. D'Holbach held his dinners on Thursdays and Sundays so they would not conflict with the Monday and Wednesday gatherings at Madame Geoffrin's home.

This wealthy, generous woman welcomed the philosophes but worried about their unbridled self-expression. She once offered a great deal of money to a friend on the condition that he burn a paper he had written. When he protested eloquently that he was unafraid, she heard him out, then asked, "How much more do you want?"

Madame Geoffrin instituted an important innovation when she subdivided her salon into two nights, each with its own character and purpose. Her Wednesday-night salon became notorious as a "fortress of free thought," thanks to the presence of philosophes and scholars, while her Monday dinners were attended by artists, art connoisseurs, and French and foreign dilettantes—people previously unwelcome in polite society.

Madame Geoffrin

Geoffrin made much of her straightforward manner and forthright style. She declared herself happy, thanks to "the truthfulness of my disposition, the naturalness of my mind, and the simplicity and variety of my tastes." Yet despite her good nature, she made enemies—rivals such as Madame du Deffand, who sought to win the philosophes to their own salons.

Madame du Deffand was neither wealthy nor particularly generous. (Her cook was known to be one of the worst in France. One guest complained that there was "only a difference of intention" between du Deffand's chef and another who had been executed for poisoning several members of the family that employed him.) But the fascinating contradictions of her personality made her magnetic. Throughout her adult life she had attacks of ennui, a kind of saturating boredom that was a common complaint of women at the time, and this made her capricious and sharp. She made friends easily but quickly abandoned them when she judged them dull. She grew as easily bored with books as with people, and professed disdain for the philosophes' ideas. Yet her salon was considered one of the most exciting in France thanks to her brilliance as a conversationalist. The salon was her only avenue of self-expression and her only distraction from the agony of boredom.

Madame du Deffand may have been no friend to the philosophes, but they had her to thank for one great gift—the introduction of Julie de Lespinasse to Parisian society. Julie was a poor, illegitimate country relative whom Madame du Deffand hired as a companion. The advanced thinkers were soon enamored of her. Where Madame du Deffand belittled them, Julie was all rapt attention.

Madame du Deffand initially enjoyed the accolades her protégée received, but later she became increasingly jealous, especially of Julie's friendship with the mathematician and philosopher d'Alembert, whom Madame du Deffand had stolen from Madame Geoffrin's circle. When du Deffand discovered that many others among her most prized guests were meeting in Julie's small rooms to talk freely before attending her own more constrained salon, she fell into a rage, saying she would "no longer feed the snake in my bosom." In 1764 she forced Julie to move out.

Julie's salon friends rallied to support her. They donated furniture and set up small pensions to keep her going. Madame Geoffrin, who had not yet met Julie but loved d'Alembert and despised du Deffand, sold three paintings from her collection to pay for Julie's apartment; they later became close friends. Julie wrote in gratitude that the mentorship first of Madame du Deffand and then of Madame Geoffrin had taught her "how to speak and how to think."

Julie de Lespinasse was plain, sickly, and too poor to feed her guests. She had no literary talent. Yet her salon thrived every evening from five to ten o'clock for twelve years. Her guests were devoted to her, perhaps because she truly loved them. The philosophes dubbed her their muse; her salon was called the "laboratory of the Encyclopedia." Philosophers, historians, and political economists mingled freely there, settling literary questions and making or breaking political reputations. People came to her small apartments to gossip, to challenge, and to be inspired. They left fired up with hope for revolution.

THE BLUESTOCKINGS OF ENGLAND: WOMEN OF PRINCIPLE

While Julie de Lespinasse and other eighteenth-century Frenchwomen made the most of their intellectual abilities, Englishwomen of this era were more reluctant to reveal their intelligence. "Learned women" in

England had to expect ridicule. It was said that women could become crazy with lust from reading. At the very least, said received opinion, they would become ill from the strain of study and were much better off devoting themselves to their husbands.

The fear of being considered too educated made women shy away from studying, lest their reputations be ruined. The learned and intelligent Lady Grey, for example, when invited to see some electrical experiments, quickly took her leave, hoping others would not think her a "*Préciuse, Femme Sçavante*, Linguist, Poetess, Mathematician, & any other name." In the end, most Englishwomen who craved education chose a middle ground: They studied, but took care to be above reproach. They shunned any hint of sexual passion and restricted their salons to literary topics.

These principled women became known as the Bluestockings. The term was coined by salon hostess Elizabeth Montague, in a joking reference to a male scholar friend who absentmindedly wore blue stockings—lower-class attire—instead of the more "respectable" white ones. The word evolved to refer to the scholarly and literary women in Montague's circle and other salons, as well as the philosophy they espoused. "Bluestocking" eventually came to mean any woman with intellectual interests.

The Bluestockings succeeded in separating learning from sin, but there was a downside to their conventionality. They looked askance at wit, and their conversation was serious, quiet, and restrained. They gave financial support to new writers (male and female), promoted the writers' work, and introduced them to publishers and critics. Male authors might deride the learned women, but they could not afford to ignore them. Perhaps most significantly, Bluestocking men and women proved that the genders could mix as equals in chaste but intellectually passionate friendship.

GERMAINE DE STAËL: A SALON IN EXILE

French salons supported social change by making it increasingly acceptable for women to receive an education, write books, choose their own sexual and marital partners, and take an active role in politics. As French society edged closer to outright revolution, a few salon women stepped into the political limelight, risking exile and execution for their beliefs. One of these women was Germaine de Staël, who grew up in a salon hosted by her mother, Madame Susanne Necker, wife of Louis XVI's influential director of finance. When Germaine was a child, her closest friends were adults such as Diderot and d'Alembert, whose ideals she took to heart; she learned the philosophy of liberation at their feet. As an adult, she was determined to be both politically involved and sexually free. Thanks to the speeches she heard from the great thinkers of

French salons supported social change by making it increasingly acceptable for women to receive an education, write books, choose their own sexual and marital partners, and take an active role in politics.

her time, Germaine acquired a lifelong taste for politics and oratory.

In 1786, when she was only twenty years old, she married the Swedish minister to France, Baron de Staël. She immediately took over her mother's salon and started a second salon at the Swedish embassy. Germaine was wealthy, idealistic, and living in a rapidly changing society. Insight, passion, imagination, theory, and oratory mattered, and she excelled at all of them.

When Germaine became pregnant with her first child by a lover, she fled to her father's home, threatening suicide rather than reconciliation

with her husband. Eventually, she won a promise from Baron de Staël that he would leave her alone for the rest of their lives—a not uncommon solution at a time when divorce was unknown.

As the French Revolution began, the revolutionaries suppressed all private gatherings, including salons. The ancien régime had considered salons inconsequential because they were run by women, and therefore ignored them, but the men of the revolutionary generation—who had plotted the overthrow of the government in women's living rooms—knew better. Every private group became suspect, and people who attended them risked denunciation, exile, or prison. Germaine fled France for the duration of the war.

Germaine de Staël

Upon her return to Paris, she was at first enthusiastic about France's new leader, Napoleon Bonaparte, but she soon realized that he was no friend of freedom and turned against him. Her reconvened salon drew all of Bonaparte's enemies, becoming a center of opposition to his policies. Napoleon understood that a salon led by a woman of Germaine's intellect and connections could destroy him, and he made it plain that anyone attending her gatherings was in danger. Germaine requested that her then-lover, the French-Swiss writer Benjamin Constant, read a speech that was extremely critical of the government. Constant warned her that it would end her social career, saying, "Your salon is filled with people who please you; if I speak tomorrow, it will be deserted. Think of it." Typically, she replied, "One must follow one's convictions." Constant was right. Her salon was empty from then on.

In 1803, Napoleon put her on a list of "permanent conspirators" and sent Germaine de Staël and Constant into exile. She fled her beloved Paris for a mansion on the shores of Lake Geneva. Heartbroken by exile, she began writing novels in which she explained her views to the public, and tried unsuccessfully to win amnesty from Napoleon. She traveled throughout Europe, and for several years held a splendid, round-the-clock salon, but Napoleon's spies hounded the gatherings and ultimately made visiting them too dangerous. Germaine remained in Swiss exile until her old enemy was himself exiled, a few years before her death in 1817.

SALONS AND THE ROMANTIC PERIOD

After the French Revolution, English men's clubs, which dated back to the fifteenth century, became the "new" model for socializing in Europe. Intentionally apolitical, they excluded women. Salons were sociable and egalitarian; club members preferred to be left alone or to cultivate convivial, shallow associations with others who were much like themselves. At the same time, women began to lose the ground they had won in French society. In the nineteenth century, Frenchwomen were not allowed to walk the streets unescorted, visit restaurants, or view sports events. Their chief means of gathering became a trivial social activity known as "the day."

Women established certain days during which they would remain at home to receive visitors. On other days, they visited other women on *their* "days." Some felt obliged to visit as many as fifty women's homes during the week. A favorite occupation on these occasions was group solitaire. Conversation lost its fire. "Days" were a burdensome round of obligations rather than a source of enlightening conversation. They eventually deteriorated to just one hour a week or a couple of hours monthly, then faded out altogether during World War II.

But with the demise of the old salon came a new kind of conversational gathering. Ambitious literary men, deprived of the once-powerful women's network, began holding their own group discussions. These men seldom planned lavish entertainment; thinking and talking mattered most in their circles. The writer Charles Nodier offered his guests only sugar-water for refreshment, candles for lighting, and the floor for seating. Nevertheless, such men became social leaders in their own right, and men have continued to host salons and other private social groups through the twentieth century.

The salon moved to the social margin, proving itself an important venue for people whose ideas or circumstances isolated them from the larger society. The groups were often run by women who were divorced, Jewish, foreign, poor, overeducated, lesbian, or known for taking a lover or offending a royal personage. Unbound by convention and shunned by society, these women felt free to welcome other inhabitants of the fringe, including artists, writers, philosophers, students, and radical politicians. The more innovators they attracted, the more exciting their salons became. These unconventional women gained an increasing degree of social influence. Nowhere was this more apparent than in the early-nineteenth-century Jewish salons of Germany.

RAHEL LEVIN: A LIGHT IN THE ATTIC

Rahel Levin lived in a tiny attic apartment in Berlin on little money, and she considered her appearance "unpleasantly unprepossessing." She deeply resented the fact that being Jewish prevented her from joining the learned society of Germany. "It is as if some supramundane being, just as I was thrust into this world," she wrote, "plunged these words with a dagger into my heart: 'Yes, have sensibility, see the world as few see it, be great and noble, nor can I take from you the faculty of eternally thinking. But I add one thing more: Be a Jewess!' And now my life is a slow bleeding to death."

Instead of surrendering, Rahel transformed her despair into a great salon. Unable to participate openly in society, she brought the world to her door. Her garret became the most sought-after meeting place of upper- and middle-class aristocrats—Jews and Christians alike—as well as actors, writers, philosophers, and emancipated women.

Rahel insisted that there be no social distinctions in her attic; only personality and intellect counted. A guest at her salon in 1801 wrote that her glance "seemed to pierce my soul. I should not have cared to meet it with a bad conscience." He goes on to describe a gathering at which the discussion touched on "the boldest ideas, the deepest thoughts, the cleverest witticisms, the most capricious fancies, all strung together by careless chit-chat. All were animated and at their ease, all seemed equally ready to listen or to talk." He was most impressed by Levin herself: "I heard from her some really inspired utterances, wonderful sayings often in a few words only, like lightning flashes, which went to one's heart."

Rahel Levin

Rahel's witty epigrams, which she called "harsh truths of the attic," were repeated throughout Germany, influencing a generation's opinions about life and art. From the time she was thirty years old until her death, Rahel Levin demonstrated that a social outsider could place herself at the center of intellectual society.

OTTOLINE AND EMERALD: SOCIETY HOSTESSES

By the start of the twentieth century, the salon took another aristocratic turn. Wealthy society hostesses opened their country homes to visitors for whole weekends, and sometimes for weeks or months in the summertime. One of these English society hostesses was Lady Ottoline Morrell. Enthusiastic young talkers gathered at her home, arguing about philosophy, human nature, politics, and literature. Bertrand Russell, Aldous Huxley, and D.H. Lawrence were regulars, and Huxley later satirized the gatherings in his novel *Crome Yellow*. Lady Ottoline recalled in her memoirs how her young guests "used to rush in on a Friday or Saturday, some by motorbikes, some by train, and crowd around the table, and then clamour for towels and bathing suits large and small, and run down to bathe in the old fish pond, and afterwards sit or lie on the lawn endlessly talking, talking. And then in the evening play games, act charades, or dance until I thought the old oak floor would fall through."

Lady Ottoline Morrell

After World War I, the most important English hostess was actually a transplanted American, born Maud Burk. When she married shipping magnate Sir Bache Cunard she changed her first name to the altogether more glamorous Emerald. At first she was ignored by proper English society women, but many later became fascinated by the novelty of an American salon in London. Lady Emerald Cunard's gatherings, which frequently lasted all weekend, were filled with journalists, explorers, scholars, sculptors, poets, and painters. Lady Emerald tolerated politicians and businessmen only if they were substantial contributors to the arts.

Harold Acton, a devoted guest, remembers Emerald Cunard as a remarkably vivacious woman who "turned conversation into champagne." (When conversation slowed, she asked her guests to sing or perform parlor tricks.) This talent, combined with her eclectic array of guests, produced "flawless occasions when poetry melted into music and music crystallized into poetry again." Nothing fazed Lady Emerald, and her ability to inspire and entertain remained intact long after she had spent her fortune supporting hungry artists and musicians. When her house was bombed during World War II, she moved into a small apartment, where, as Harold Acton recalled, "the war was all around us, bursting and crashing above and below; yet it failed to penetrate that seventh-floor apartment or pollute the conversation."

CONVERSATIONS IN PRAGUE AND MADRID

Discussion groups also proliferated elsewhere in Europe in the early twentieth century. Beginning in 1921, for example, the Patecnici ("Friday Men") gathered weekly at five o'clock in novelist and playwright

Karel Capek's home in Prague. Originally devoted to art and literature, the salon was so diverse that topics soon included science and politics. The multilingual Capek invited people from many countries, putting them at ease by talking to them in their own languages. If the conversation stalled, Capek invariably introduced a new subject—the virtues or defects of a new art movement, the state of the Czech republic, modern physics—guaranteed to stir up his guests.

Prague's numerous coffeehouses were famous for their literary conversation between World War I and World War II. The Devetsil group of poets and painters, staunch modernists, held fiery discussions in the Cafe Union and the Cafe Slavia, while the more sedate Arco and the Louvre attracted Franz Kafka and other Prague literati of German language and culture.

In Spain, groups called *tertulias* closely paralleled salons, and they remain standard social fare in Spain and Latin America today. Tertulias sprang up in the eighteenth century as intellectuals and nobility gathered in private homes to talk. By the early nineteenth century, they had spread to the middle class and were held in cafés and the offices of literary magazines. One of the first public tertulias was an antimonarchist revolutionary group that met at the Fontana de Oro, the Golden Foun-

La Tertulia del Café de Pombo (1920), a painting of the Pombo salon in Madrid, by José Gutiérrez Solana. Ramón Gómez de la Serna is the standing figure.

tain café, in Madrid. In his comic novel of the same name, Benito Pérez Galdós describes one of the problems associated with holding revolutionary salons in public places:

> The radicals pigeonholed themselves in The Golden Fountain, and those who were not radicals were driven out. Finally, it was decided that the sessions would be secret, so the club was moved upstairs. Those who were seated below were paying customers, drinking coffee or chocolate; they heard the frightening uproar from above in the heated moments of discussion and some, fearing that the ceiling would cave in on them along with the whole political heap, took to the hills, abandoning their inveterate custom of frequenting the café.

Probably the best-known twentieth-century tertulia is the one frequented by the beloved Spanish author Ramón Gómez de la Serna, who met with his friends for decades at the Pombo café in Madrid. Writers and artists gathered every Saturday night to talk, doodle cartoons, read each other's manuscripts, and write. Some came by personal invitation; others dropped by out of curiosity as the fame of the Pombo tertulia spread. Eventually Latin American writers and artists, including the poet Pablo Neruda, the fabulist Jorge Luis Borges, and the muralist Diego Rivera, found their way to the artistic haven of the Pombo, with its vociferous discussions and carnivalesque atmosphere—and to Ramón, its imaginative, energetic, mercurial focal point. The Pombo salon came to a sad end: the Spanish Civil War and Ramón's consequent exile to Argentina in 1936. The fate of the most memorable of all tertulias is another example of the vexed relationship between politics and conversation.

CHAPTER TWO

CONVERSATION AMERICAN STYLE:

EARLY 1900s TO THE PRESENT

J ust as modern American literature and art were midwifed in Europe—in Ezra Pound's Italy, T.S. Eliot's London, Virgil Thomson's Paris—the modern American salon got its start on the old continent, too: in Paris and Florence, thanks to two of the most remarkable women of the early twentieth century, Gertrude Stein and Mabel Dodge.

GERTRUDE STEIN: PARIS CONVERSATIONS

Paris' reputation as the cultural capital of the West, which began in the seventeenth century, culminated in the first half of the twentieth, when the city on the Seine was nursemaid to the modern art movement. As the century turned, Paris was an obligatory stop on the global pilgrimage of writers, artists, propagandists, and patrons of the new aesthetic. The versatile writer Gertrude Stein was also a salonist of genius, and at the heart of the early-twentieth-century cultural revolution.

The Stein home at 27 rue de Fleurus—shared by Gertrude, her brother, Leo, and eventually Gertrude's lover and collaborator, Alice B. Toklas—was a stopover for virtually every art-minded visitor to Paris from before World War I through the 1920s. The salon came about because these visitors kept dropping in at unpredictable hours to see the collection of modern art owned by Gertrude and Leo, who were pioneer patrons of postimpressionism and the even more radical movements spawned by it, such as cubism. Gertrude was struggling with her long prose work, *The Making of Americans.* "It was not to be written with people coming and going at all hours," she later wrote, "and so the Saturday evenings evolved out of necessity and only after nine o'clock."

At the appointed hour, Gertrude would show people into the studio. There, Leo would entertain them with long expositions on Picasso, Matisse, Gauguin, and the other little-known painters whose work he collected. Gertrude described the crowd as coming in "all sizes and shapes, all degrees of wealth and poverty, some very charming, some simply rough and every now and then a very beautiful young peasant. Then there were quantities of Germans, not too popular because they tended

Gertrude Stein, by Man Ray

always to want to see anything that was put away and they tended to break things. . . . Then there was a fair sprinkling of Americans . . . some painters and occasionally an architecture student would accidentally get there . . . people came and went, in and out."

Like many good salonkeepers, Gertrude remained in the background, rarely asserting herself but making her presence felt and setting the tone for a pleasant evening of conversation. New York journalist and frequent salon guest Hutchins Hapgood described Gertrude as "generally silent, but with a deep warmth that expressed itself in her handclasp, her look, and her rich laughter."

Gertrude's opinions, when she offered them, were sharp and clear. She might chat with her close friend H.P. Roche, a Parisian man-about-town whom she called "a general introducer." Not only did Roche, who had been everywhere in Europe, contribute cosmopolitan invitees to the gatherings, but he helped give Gertrude a sense of her vocation. "One day Gertrude Stein said something about herself," writes Stein herself in *The Autobiography of Alice B. Toklas,* "and Roche said good good excellent that is very important for your biography. She was terribly touched, it was the first time that she really realised that some time she would have a biography." With Matisse she chatted amiably, and with painter Andre Derain she argued violently, over philosophy and the merits of Goethe's *Faust.* She could also be very funny, and visitors invariably commented on her beautiful contralto laugh. In her openness to visitors, her willingness to welcome anyone and everyone, Gertrude Stein kept faith with the traditional salon.

MABEL DODGE: VILLA CURONIA TO NEW YORK

Buffalo-born Mabel Dodge began life as a typical female product of the Gilded Age. Born to wealth, married (after her first husband died in a hunting accident) to a prosperous Boston society architect, she was a would-be patroness of the arts with a penchant for the Italian Renaissance. But when she and husband Edwin Dodge actually went to Florence to live in 1905, the stage was set for her transformation into a salonkeeping muse of the modern.

With her husband's help, she transformed the ruinous Villa Curonia, a fifteenth-century estate, into a sort of dream palace with a festive French-style sitting room, a somber neomedieval bedroom, and galleries beautified with the fruits of her many buying sprees. In the midst of it all she installed herself, attired in brocaded gowns and turbans like a Medici princess, and began inviting a fascinating cross section of native and expatriate Florentine society to salon evenings. The titled and the ostracized mixed at the Villa Curonia: artists, homosexuals, political exiles, the great Italian actress Eleanora Duse (recovering rather operatically from

an affair with the world-famous, and famously megalomaniacal, Italian poet Gabriele D'Annunzio), the art historian and connoisseur Bernard Berenson. Berenson's wife, Mary, was uncomfortable in this mixed company: "Mabel Dodge made friends with all the people in Florence whom we consider peculiarly undesirable," she sniffed. But this formidably miscellaneous Tuscan salon was just a foretaste of the excitement Dodge would stir up later.

Mabel, whose libidinous impulses had been awakened at Villa Curonia along with her artistic ones, soon left the tepid Edwin and went to New York. A five-story house at 23 Fifth Avenue became her new showplace and salon.

Mabel Dodge at Villa Curonia

In 1913 she met Carl Van Vechten, an Iowa-born aesthete and journalist who was well-connected in Manhattan art and new-thought circles. Soon evenings at 23 Fifth were enlivened by Van Vechten's invitees: Broadway actresses and dancers from Harlem, poets, playwrights, gossipmongers. Hutchins Hapgood, a tireless promoter of new ideas in art, literature, and leftist politics, shared Dodge's interest in mysticism but found her "completely innocent of the world of labor and of revolution in politics, art, and industry"—and eager to learn. He began to bring an assortment of dodgy characters to her salons. As Max Eastman (editor of the radical newspaper *The Masses*, who didn't care for salons or for Mabel) later put it, "A cult arose among them of making friends with criminals."

Thieves and murderers, New York's intellectual elite, the unemployed, strikers and scabs, wealthy poseurs, socialists, unionists, anarchists, and suffragettes, poets, lawyers, artists, psychics, government officials, and psychoanalysts—all were welcome at Mabel's "evenings." Birth control advocate Margaret Sanger recalled: "Their clothes may have been unkempt, but their eyes were ablaze with interest and intelligence. . . . Each knew his own side of the subject as well as any scholar. You had to inform yourself to be in the liberal movement. Ideas were respected, but you had to back them up with facts."

> Thieves and murderers, New York's intellectual elite, the unemployed, socialists, unionists, anarchists, and suffragettes, poets, lawyers, artists, psychics, government officials, and psychoanalysts—all were welcome at Mabel's "evenings."

Once Mabel had established a topic or asked a speaker to start with a short lecture, she rarely said anything. Plain, plump, and silent, she attracted others through what Max Eastman described as a "magnetic field in which people become polarized and pulled in and made to behave very queerly. Their passions become exacerbated; they grow argumentative; they have quarrels, difficulties, entanglements, abrupt and violent detachments. And they like it—they come back for more."

Mabel explained the popularity of her evenings more modestly, saying they simply filled an empty niche in New York's social scene:

> There were so many people with things to say, and so few places to say them in. There seemed to be no centralization in New York, no meeting place for free exchange of ideas and talk. So many interesting people only meeting each other in print! So I thought I would try to get people together a little and see if it wouldn't increase understanding if they would all talk among themselves and say what they thought. And I think I did. . . . Some who had been enemies for years in the hateful half-truth of newspaper columns came more and more to understand one another as they aired their views together in the open.

The group that gathered for her salons lent their weight to a whole range of causes, including women's suffrage, modern art, and organized labor. Perhaps the most memorable political-artistic adventure involving salon members was an elaborate pageant in support of striking silk workers in Paterson, New Jersey, in 1913. The labor extravaganza, which brought a thousand real silk workers on stage to recreate the strike in the old Madison Square Garden on Madison Avenue, was masterminded by radical journalist John Reed, with sets by prominent avant-garde scene designer Robert Trent Jones. A wildly enthusiastic audience of workers turned the performance into a union meeting, complete with a rousing rendition of the *Internationale* at the end.

The show galvanized leftist and liberal popular opinion on behalf of the strikers, and journalists swarmed to Paterson to cover the real strike. The pageant, with its powerful scene design and cacaphonous industrial "noise-music" influenced by Italian futurism, had just as powerful an effect on the theater world. Playwrights George Cram Cook and Susan Glaspell stayed up all night after the show, arguing and dreaming about what American theater could become. In a few years, the pair would found the Provincetown Playhouse, where the works of Eugene O'Neill would premiere, pushing American theater into the modern era.

On occasion, Mabel's lust for experimentation led to awkwardness or worse. An evening devoted to a discussion of sexual equality ended abruptly when a young woman endorsed free love by announcing that she was available to any man in the room. On another night, eight of Mabel's friends ingested some peyote supplied by an anthropologist friend who studied Native American ritual. For a time the effect was very pleasant and mysterious, as the friends serenely meditated and chanted. But the evening ended in disaster when one girl became frightened and ran out of the building. The rest spent the night hunting for her, and finally telegraphed her father to tell him his daughter had suffered a nervous breakdown.

Mabel left New York in 1917. Wartime suspicion of unconventional activity had made her gatherings increasingly dangerous, and she had received threats from the police. (Later, some of her friends were tried for sedition or deported.) She moved to Taos, New Mexico, where her home became a magnet for the likes of Georgia O'Keeffe and D.H. Lawrence, and the iconoclastic spirit of her salonkeeping years matured into serenity and spiritual calm.

THE ALGONQUIN ROUND TABLE: WIT IN PUBLIC

One of the most famous salons ever to be held was made up of a group of acidulous creative personalities including writers Dorothy Parker and Alexander Woollcott, humorist Robert Benchley, actor Alfred Lunt, novelist Edna Ferber, playwright George S. Kaufman, and columnist/drama critic Heywood Broun. These sophisticates met for lunch nearly every day from 1920 until the early 1930s at the Algonquin Hotel in New York City. Frank Case, the manager and later owner of the hotel, eventually provided them with their own large, round table in the hotel's Rose Room, and the group, known informally as the Vicious Circle, was soon dubbed the Algonquin Round Table by journalistic colleagues.

These were young, hungry thinkers with acid tongues, boundless ambitions, and high standards of craft. They attacked the objects of their disesteem with unrelenting humor, and their witticisms were widely quoted (and misquoted). True children of the sharp and rather cynical twenties, they waged war on sentimentality, particularly in writing. *Lovely, sweet, nice, terrible,* and *awful* were among the lazy words they

The Algonquin Round Table, by Al Hirschfeld. Clockwise around the table, from left: Dorothy Parker, Robert Benchley, Alexander Woollcott, Heywood Broun, Marc Connelly, Franklin P. Adams, Edna Ferber, George S. Kaufman, Robert Sherwood. Top left to right: Lynn Fontanne, Alfred Lunt, Frank Crowninshield, and Algonquin Hotel manager Frank Case.

couldn't abide. They could also be rough on each other. One day Heywood Broun arrived for lunch inveighing against what he took to be abuse of the word *wistful* in the public prints. "I keep reading about this 'wistful' novel, this 'wistful' bit of nostalgia," he said. "If they have to be 'wistful' why can't they get a book of synonyms and look up a good clean name for it?"

It was the wrong thing to say to the formidable Woollcott, de facto leader of the Round Table and multifarious man of letters. *Wistful* was one of his all-time favorite words, and he was hurt. He looked daggers at the rumpled, perpetually boyish Broun.

"Coming from one who, during his entire adult life, has bumped along on the flay wheel of wistfulness," snapped Woollcott, "I find this capsule critique ill-advised."

The Round Table tended to stick together even when they weren't lunching at the Algonquin, gathering at the theater or in one another's apartments to play poker or charades. Playwright Noel Coward, taken aback after running into the entire group three times at three different places in the course of a single day, remarked, "But don't they ever see anyone bloody else?" Although they plainly preferred their own company, they gladly welcomed new people into the group, provided they could keep up with the humor and worked at their craft diligently.

The members of the Round Table eagerly took up one another's causes. The women were ardently in favor of women's suffrage; some of them wrote and demonstrated for the cause. They expected the men to treat them as equals, with exactly the same standards of friendship and camaraderie. Broun and others in the group with leftist sympathies promoted the cause of organized labor and rallied to the defense of anarchist martyrs Sacco and Vanzetti.

Increasing fame, heavier workloads, and the ordinary ups and downs of life eventually separated the group. But while it lasted, it was a true salon—eclectic, creative, and democratic.

THE HARLEM RENAISSANCE: SALONS, DANCES, AND SUPPERS

Just as Jews in Germany found a social outlet in conversational gatherings, so African Americans in New York found in salons an effective way to exchange ideas and support one another. While many white American artists and writers fled to Paris, black Americans were busy asserting their culture and literature in the United States. Their salons were as varied as any in history. Langston Hughes recalled that "at the James Weldon Johnson parties and gumbo suppers, one met solid people like Clarence and Mrs. Darrow. At Dr. Alexander's, you met the upper-crust Negro intellectuals like Dr. DuBois. At Wallace Thurman's, you met the bohemians of both Harlem and the Village. And in the gin mills and speakeasies and night clubs between 125th and 145th, Eighth Avenue and Lenox, you met everybody."

Lana Turner, a salonkeeper living in Harlem today, recalls that the Harlem salons of the 1920s "were full of the painters of the day, the musicians of the day, the writers of the day. Not only did they come together to talk about their work, they did it so often and so frequently and informally, it was tantamount to borrowing sugar next door."

A'Lelia Walker Robinson

Sometimes they ended up at hair-straightening heiress A'Lelia Walker Robinson's mansion at Irvington-on-the-Hudson for lavish, upper-crust parties or the literary salon called the Dark Tower that she held on the upper floor of her house. At writer Jessie Fauset's home, there were evenings of talking literature, reading poetry aloud, and conversing in French. The get-togethers allowed salonists to escape from white faddists "momentarily in love with Negro life," as Langston Hughes put it in his autobiography.

But the center of the Harlem Renaissance was writer and poet Wallace Thurman's apartment on 136th Street. In Hughes' portrayal, Thurman was gifted with the intriguing contradictions of a Madame du Deffand or a Rahel Levin. He was "a strange kind of fellow, who liked to drink gin, but didn't like to drink gin," Hughes wrote. He "liked being a Negro, but felt it a great handicap; [he] adored bohemianism, but thought it wrong to be a bohemian. He liked to waste a lot of time, but he always felt guilty wasting time. He loathed crowds, yet he hated to be alone. He almost always felt bad, yet he didn't write poetry." Some of Harlem's most important writers—and all of Harlem's young hopefuls—flocked to his house, leading Thurman and novelist-ethnologist Zora Neale Hurston to refer to the salon mockingly as "Niggerati manor."

This was probably the last time in history when salons blossomed as part of a whole community, as a single dimension of social life among friends who regularly worked and played together. All of Harlem was a setting and an inspiration to the writers. The importance of the problems to be discussed, the volatile and vital mood of the place, the sense the participants had of being part of a significant group at a time of meaningful change—these elements were the fertile soil of the Harlem scene, as they have been for all great salons.

Harlem get-togethers allowed salonists to escape from white faddists "momentarily in love with Negro life," as Langston Hughes puts it in his autobiography.

CONTEMPORARY SALONS: HERE, THERE, THEN EVERYWHERE

During the social disruptions of the Great Depression and World War II, salons became virtually extinct as a regular social activity. The word itself fell into disuse—except, of course, to indicate a place where women get their hair done. Many discussion groups were spawned in the 1960s and 1970s, but they were limited in scope and different in tone from the salon. Most had an agenda for specific political or social change and concentrated more on tactics than on ideas. And the personal-growth groups that appeared in the 1970s for the most part had a narrower focus than the freewheeling salons of the great tradition.

Nevertheless, a few people maintained the tradition, usually with a circle of friends who were artistic or wealthy or both. Luba Petrova Harrington held a salon during the 1960s in her New York apartment. Writer John Berendt remembers her "ability to draw even the most reticent grump into lively conversation." Her lively group of regular guests included former king Peter of Yugoslavia, *New Yorker* cartoonist Charles Addams, Doubleday president John Sargent, *Harper's* editor Willie Morris, jazz bassist Charlie Mingus, and "assorted artists, writers, hippies, movie directors, blue bloods, and deadbeats." Harrington, a plump, forceful, but motherly woman who had lived the jet-set life in Rome and taught Russian at Yale, brought a unique combination of sharp wit and unpretentiousness to salonkeeping. When Timothy Leary, a frequent guest, kissed her hand and declared her the "leading *saloniste* in New York," she replied genially, "Doctor Leary, you are full of shit, as usual."

Even in this period, salonists proved that any group that meets regularly can become a salon without much forethought. The Thinkers and Drinkers, a salon in New Jersey that lasted nearly ten years, got its start in the early 1960s when friends at a cocktail party remarked that "we never really talk." Four couples decided to start meeting for discussion, each taking a turn at hosting and choosing the evening's topic. Cofounder Barbara Neal, now in her seventies, recalls that "after a few years, we knew what everybody thought about everything." To liven things up, the Thinkers and Drinkers began to invite guest speakers and guest couples.

On the other side of the country, the Friday Morning Conversation Group got under way during the same years. Cofounder Carolyn Wardner Buck recalled it in a 1992 letter to *Utne Reader:*

> We were a vastly diverse group, including a Ph.D. psychologist, a film editor, a book publisher, teachers, activists, and homemakers. We met for three hours every Friday morning, rotating from home to home among the members who had domiciles large enough to accommodate the group and their children, for whom we hired two on-scene baby-sitters to keep them safely occupied nearby but out of the range of the conversations.
>
> Our conversations ranged widely from homosexuality, prayer in public schools, local issues confronting candidates for city offices, bodies of work by an author, the historical, biological, and social roles of women, etc., etc. We had no by-laws or officers except for the one rule that if a participant stated something as fact, it should be provable, or if opinion, labeled as opinion. . . . We steered away from 'guest speakers,' except for an occasional representative from a group such as the Mattachine Society (male homosexuals seeking to achieve legislatively their human rights) or all of the candidates for Los Angeles City Council (who all came eagerly, and who participated fully). We never discussed a book, but always the body of work by an author, seeking to discover commonalities, style, and growth from book to book.
>
> That Friday Morning Conversation Group was the most memorable ongoing experience of my life, and some of my lifelong friendships were made in it.

In the early 1970s, activist and ecologist Stephanie Mills received a Point Foundation grant to hold a salon in Stockholm during the U.N. Conference on the Human Environment, where "ecofreaks," poets (Gary Snyder and Michael McClure), residents of the Hog Farm commune, Native American and white members of the Black Mesa Defense Fund, and other activists were arriving from the United States for environmental consciousness-raising. "All I wanted to do was give dinner parties," Mills admits. "Almost within minutes, funding was available for me to join the gang and set up the salon." In Stockholm, she hosted a number of salons built around environmental topics.

Stephanie Mills

Back at home in Berkeley, Mills once again got funds from the Point Foundation, this time to "bring people together who wouldn't necessarily meet, to provide them with a leisurely, gracious environment in which to become acquainted and intelligently converse, to encourage skylarking." Her account of these salons, published in *CoEvolution Quarterly* magazine, planted the seed for the rebirth of salons throughout the United States in the 1990s.

Eric Utne, then a young editor, was impressed by Mills' article. He especially liked the word *salon*, with its historical associations and the combined implication of glamour and revolution. He soon started what he called New Age salons—irregular parties that enabled print and broadcast journalists to, in his words, "meet their peers and schmooze." These get-togethers were not so much true salons as overcrowded parties, fifty to a hundred people in a large room, but they affirmed Utne's notion that "bringing people together and getting them to talk about the stuff they care about and believe in" is important and enjoyable.

He returned to the salon idea in 1984, as he was starting his new magazine, *Utne Reader*. This time he asked "certified media junkies from various perspectives" to read a number of alternative publications, then gather once a month to talk about what to reprint in the magazine. Soon he realized that the salonists were more fascinating than what they were reading. "I began asking them what they were thinking and obsessing about," he says. "That question seemed to trigger some interesting conversations." The *Utne Reader* Alternative Press Reading and Dining Salon became a way of "tapping into the zeitgeist," as Utne puts it, and a continual source of new ideas for the magazine.

Utne took modern salons a giant step further when a 1991 issue of *Utne Reader* included several articles on salons, and a small advertisement invited readers to "meet up to twenty-five other people in your neighborhood (town, bioregion)" by starting or joining a salon, a study circle, or a council. Readers who sent in their names and addresses would receive, without charge, a list of people with the same zip code who were equally interested in forming a salon.

The response was staggering. Within a few months, 8,000 people had joined the *Utne* salons. Within sixteen months, 13,000 people had signed up. With the help of a grant from the Surdna Foundation, *Utne Reader* formed the community-service-oriented Neighborhood Salon Association to handle the paperwork. The NSA and the magazine published a small pamphlet, "The Salon-keeper's Companion," and periodic newsletters to help salon members organize their gatherings.

By August 1993, over 20,000 people had signed up and formed more than 325 salons nationwide. Dozens of newspaper and magazine articles noted the phenomenon, and many other organizations began holding discussion groups among their members, readers, or listeners. As Utne had hoped, the salon concept quickly spread far beyond readers of the magazine.

Whether people were looking for friends, anticipating debate, or just wanting new experiences, salons clearly addressed a need they had not articulated until they envisioned the possibility of vital, meaningful conversation. The modern American salon is really just one meeting place among many, one part of the movement to regain our sense of community and to bring people back into democratic participation in local and national affairs. This is the task of the next century—one that has just begun. Every person who has taken the risk of starting a conversational group is now making history, by joining and furthering a great tradition.

PART TWO

FOUNDATIONS: GETTING YOUR SALON STARTED

CHAPTER THREE

GETTING ORGANIZED:
FIRST STEPS

Why not organize all this accidental, unplanned activity around you,
this coming and going of visitors, and see these people at certain hours.
Have Evenings! . . . Get people here at certain times and let them feel
absolutely free to be themselves, and see what happens. Let everybody
come! All these different kinds of people that you know, together here,
without being managed or herded in any way! Something wonderful
might come of it! You might even revive General Conversation!
~ Journalist Lincoln Steffens to salonkeeper Mabel Dodge

The classic salons came into being easily. A great lady—a Madame du Deffand or a Rahel Levin—simply spread the word through court or literary circles that she would be at home on a given night, and, beginning with the lady's closest friends, the circle began to assemble. In their heyday, so much magic and glamour surrounded certain salons that everyone who wasn't intimidated by the circle of invitees wanted in. Nor did the salongoers of the past find it necessary to debate the merits of structure or spontaneity in their salons. The salons were run by individuals with a clear social vision, in a stratified culture that knew precisely what behavior was appropriate.

Salons rarely arise so spontaneously in our busy, complicated, egalitarian day and age. Someone must be willing to arrange the time, the place, and what will happen at that time and place. The least complicated way of setting up a salon is for one person to make all the initial decisions. This person needs to be organized, socially savvy, and energetic, with a healthy ego, a reasonably sized living room, a number of friends, and plenty of entertaining ideas. The leader's personality, needs, and interests will determine the mood and goals of the salon, and the number of people it attracts will depend upon how inspiring they find the leader's vision.

And yet, in this scenario, the leader will end up doing all or most of the work himself (let's say this salonkeeper is a man). By the time the salon begins, he may be worn out from making the preparations, or so busy trying to put everyone at ease that he never relaxes and enjoys himself. He may overcompensate by trying to exert greater control over how others participate, and risk losing members when people begin to resent his newly minted rules. If a particular evening disappoints, the leader may feel so discouraged that he's reluctant to continue the salon.

In most cases, sharing the decisions and preparations with a core group of people is more viable. When a small group makes the decisions, negotiations can proceed quickly. The group process creates a reliable base of members who continue to share responsibility. Anyone who joins the salon later has agreed, in a sense, to abide by the standards and structure set up by the initial group. It's a good idea to spell out your plans at the first salon session, asking everyone for suggestions and preferences.

One disadvantage to this approach is that salons run by a group sometimes lack the overriding vision and resolve that a single, inspired person can bring to the task of keeping a salon in motion—after all, there's no substitute for a Julie de Lespinasse or a Mabel Dodge. And if the core group is perceived as an elite in-group, unresponsive to the wishes of other salon members, there may be quiet attrition as disaffected prospects fall away and the salon dwindles. Then, if members of the core group leave, the salon is in real danger of petering out.

One solution is to invite everyone who's expressed interest in the salon to help plan it. Salons that begin with the full participation of all members tend to last the longest and develop the greatest intimacy. They often generate the most innovative organizational ideas and are the most likely to extend into relationships outside the salon.

Not that trying to accommodate the views and desires of two dozen people is easy. The negotiations can be so difficult that the salon never gets organized. It may take two or three sessions to hash out the details, and people without the stomach for negotiation may quit in disgust. If you choose to accelerate the process by voting rather than trying to achieve consensus, you may lose people who feel that their concerns are being ignored. In most cases, only a few people have the energy and commitment necessary for running a salon, and these people end up forming a core group anyway.

Each of these start-up methods can work with the right group of people, but, at least in our day, salons started by small groups tend to get off the ground most efficiently and amicably. For purposes of discussion, we'll assume that structure in what follows.

THE FIRST MEETING

The salon's first meeting is more than an opportunity for its members to get to know one another. It's also the time to ask some fundamental questions: What kind of salon will this be? When and where will it meet? Will food be served? How will the salon handle expenses? How can it build membership? How should topics be chosen? Who's in charge of what? Arriving at thoughtful answers to these questions can

"The Sculleys, the Jensons, the Walkers, Freddy, Joan, Don, and the Bowes. Oh, well, Madame de Staël had to start somewhere."

make future organizational meetings easier, or even unnecessary. This is more than enough territory to cover in one meeting. If you feel that it is necessary to set ground rules for salon interactions, you might schedule a second meeting specifically to discuss group dynamics.

The first meeting inevitably sets a tone for the salon, so it's wise to keep it as informal as possible, with time for socializing and plenty of breaks. Following introductions, you might ask each person to answer two or three questions, such as:

- Why do you want to be in a salon?
- What do you hope will emerge from the salon in the future?
- What other groups have you participated in, and how would you like this one to be different?

However the questions are phrased, the aim is to get an overview of the group's philosophy and expectations. Gauge whether the group prefers a high degree of structure or would rather be as casual as possible. Do people want to remain acquaintances who share conversation, or do they hope to make friends and form a community? Do they prefer a straightforward discussion group, or are they open to other activities and outings?

It's not necessary for everyone in the group to share the same expectations—nor is it likely that they will. The idea is for everyone to hear a variety of perspectives and possibilities. This initiates the process of binding the members together, which in turn simplifies the practical decisions that follow.

Next begins the process of arriving at consensus and adopting, through discussion, a format that everyone can live with. You may want to talk about alternatives to general conversation salons, such as study circles, councils, and creativity salons, which are explained in a later chapter. Many salons combine aspects of all of them and vary their focus over time. When you have decided in a broad sense what kind of salon you want, your group is ready to make practical arrangements.

WHEN? HOW OFTEN?

Early salons were conducted in a culture of leisure that gave participants time to meet daily, or to spend time together for weeks or months on end in country mansions. Madame Geoffrin became famous for adding to her Wednesday salon—largely literary and philosophical—a Monday gathering to which she invited painters and musicians. Indeed, hosting salons was very nearly a full-time profession for the great ladies of the eighteenth century, and going to salons was a regular part of the job description for ambitious writers and artists. Nowadays, though, we have to squeeze salons in. Most working people and parents consider even a weekly commitment too much of a strain on their schedules. Consequently, most modern salons meet once or twice a month.

A monthly meeting is the easiest to set up and works best for most start-up salons. Choose a day of the month—the third Tuesday, the first Friday—and stick to it. Most salons meet weekday evenings after work. Some salons meet Sunday afternoons. Very few meet on Saturdays, because a Saturday session seems to fragment the weekend.

Meeting less frequently than once a month undermines continuity and often prevents the group from cohering into a salon. The meeting may instead resemble an irregular party. An exception to the rule is a group that already exists in another context, such as a business or church group that wants to add salon conversations to its other activities.

If your group seems intent on building a circle of friends and developing a sense of community, you may decide to meet weekly. Weekly salons reinforce continuity and intimacy. At the same time, they are generally rather informal: less concerned about sending out invitations, deciding on topics, being prompt, and so on. While you might expect fewer people to show up weekly, the opposite is often true, because people more readily remember to come to frequent gatherings.

Many weekly salons taper off after a year or two, deciding at that point to hold monthly gatherings. People who have established friendships find themselves getting together outside the salon, so they no longer need frequent meetings to support their connections. Other salons start out holding monthly meetings, then increase the frequency as they grow more involved in their conversations. One Connecticut group found that the salon was split between people who wanted to see each other often and others who didn't have the time to meet more than once a month. They responded by scheduling one constant, "official" meeting for the last Monday of each month, and another informal session arranged by those who wanted to get together more frequently.

Think twice about starting your salon during the summer months. In many parts of the country, people are busy with family outings, vacations, gardening, sports, and other outdoor activities. It's often best to start a salon in early autumn or late winter, when schedules are more stable and people are amenable to being indoors.

WHAT TIME? HOW LONG?

Most contemporary salons must accommodate nine-to-five work schedules. Getting together at around seven or eight in the evening on a weeknight generally works best. You can assume that most people have had dinner before coming, but providing snacks can help keep those who have not eaten focused on the conversation.

You may wish to consider variables such as weather and daylight. Some salons vary their schedules seasonally, meeting early all winter and late evenings in the summer, to avoid spending too much time indoors when the weather is pleasant. In general, you can expect your membership to fall off during the summer months. Some salons opt to shut down altogether during July and August, while others plan a single weekend trip or hold daytime barbecues instead of their usual evening meetings.

Avoid setting limits on how long you'll stay. Allow at least two hours for conversation, but be willing to go for as long as three or four if the rhythm of the conversation demands it, and if the hosts and other salonists are agreeable. Still, judge the group's curve of energy carefully and don't let things run down before ending. It's always better to call a halt while the salon is still bubbling with ideas and excitement.

One highly successful salon ran only sixty to ninety minutes on Saturday mornings. Short salons encourage brevity and sticking to the point. They can produce fast-moving, stimulating conversations. But because they don't allow time for socializing, they also reduce the likelihood of forming friendships. They are often run in a rather businesslike, controlled fashion. Some people may not get a chance to speak, and rarely will the conversations probe as deeply into a topic as those in more relaxed salons.

Annual weekend retreat of the Washington Area Artists' Salon on Antietam Creek, Maryland

If your salon lasts for more than a couple of hours, you may drift off the topic or get physically restless. It can be helpful to break up long conversations with snacks or other activities. Conversations that seem exhausted often pick up after a break. During the first half of a conversation, people tend to air their preconceived opinions and theories, feeling that they have now said all there is to be said. If they have time to think over the comments of others, however, they often return to the conversation with new insights, greater willingness to reveal themselves, and eagerness to deal with the subject at a more complex and subtle level. Longer conversations allow more time for frivolity, too. People with a little time on their hands are more likely to joke around, swap movie and book reviews, or listen to a new CD that someone has brought along.

Setting a regular meeting time, one that rarely if ever varies, is almost imperative. Start-up salons should select a fixed day and time, at least until the membership stabilizes and communications are in place. If you vary your meeting schedule in an effort to accommodate everyone, many members will be unable to remember the day and time you settled upon.

The drawback of a fixed, invariable meeting time is that some people who would like to attend your salon may never be able to make it. One solution is to alternate days regularly. This can work if you maintain regular contact with all members through a newsletter or similar device, and if the meetings are fairly frequent—at least biweekly—so people who can't attend on a particular day don't have to wait two months to resume their participation.

> "Our talk began with luncheon, reached a climax at tea, and by dinner we were staggering with it. By five o'clock in the morning we were unconscious but still talking," wrote poet Margaret Anderson about her 1920s salon.

"Our talk began with luncheon, reached a climax at tea, and by dinner we were staggering with it. By five o'clock in the morning we were unconscious but still talking," wrote poet Margaret Anderson about her 1920s salon. Imitate her by spending an entire day or weekend together at least once a year, so you'll have an opportunity to participate in extended, virtually limitless conversation. Talking retreats allow conversations to continue far into the night and draw a group closer together, so that regular meetings are likely to become friendlier, more heartfelt, and more deeply truthful.

THE PERILS OF PROMPTNESS

Attitudes toward latecomers can be a real sticking point in some salons. It's important to realize that expectations about promptness are cultural and personal, not universal. Even in the clock-conscious culture of the United States, many people consider it polite to be fashionably late, feeling that tardiness allows the hosts more time to prepare. Some people make distinctions between formal occasions, when you should arrive on the dot, and casual get-togethers, which are looser.

Mandatory promptness means there's a power dynamic in operation—someone in authority demands your timely presence. Not ringing the tardy bell, on the other hand, signals that the group members are all equals, and each life is as important as the next. Even so, the thread of the discussion can be lost for minutes at a time as a latecomer is introduced, and sometimes the original momentum is never regained. What to do? You can simply set aside the first fifteen minutes to an hour for socializing. (This also gives your host a little more time to set things up.) By the time the "official" discussion begins, everyone will generally have arrived, and the small talk will have put everyone at ease. This strategy can be especially useful for groups that are having trouble attracting enough members to meetings. If you don't have picky tardiness rules, you're likely to attract and hold more people. For everyone, the salon will feel more like a pleasurable outing than an obligation.

A break midway through the meeting comes highly recommended too, as it gives late arrivals a chance to mingle and introduce themselves. These measures make it unnecessary to interrupt the salon conversation for latecomers, and talk can flow on unimpeded.

FOOD AND DRINK

"Probably there had never been such a mingling of art, sex, politics, spiritualism, cold meats, and lettuce sandwiches," wrote Oscar Carghill, describing Mabel Dodge's New York salon before World War I. By that time, salon food had become decidedly informal, at least by comparison to the fare offered by the President Henault, dear friend of Madame du Deffand and doyen of his own salon. Prepared by the great chef Legrange, this grand cuisine was the president's calling card in an age of great, and fiercely competitive, salons.

Modern salons often serve snacks and beverages or potluck meals. The long-lived Cincinnati RADS (Reading and Dining Society) salon begins with a potluck dinner at six, with discussion at seven. A number of the salon's members are first-rate cooks. "We feel very strongly about food," says member Daniel Hadley. "In fact, we are certain that food has kept our group together while others in the area have failed." A full meal at the beginning of a salon can make people too sluggish for lively conversation; on the other hand, they may get impatient or restless if they are hungry. Food can provide a gratifying break in the middle of a meeting, and it may ease the transition to a different activity or conversational mode. "When throats grew dry and the flood of oratory waned," early-twentieth-century feminist Margaret Sanger said of her salon, "someone went out for hamburger sandwiches, hot dogs, and beer, paid for by all. . . . These considerate friends never imposed a burden either of extra work or extra expense. In the kitchen everyone sliced, buttered, opened cans. As soon as all were refreshed, the conversation was resumed practically where it had left off."

In certain cases, food can underscore the salon's theme, as it did for the now-defunct WOWEE (Women of the World Eating Everything) group

The Tracy's Tertulia, a writers' salon in Minneapolis.
Coauthor Jon Spayde is third from right.

in New York. The group met in monthly gatherings organized around a country or another geographical area. A book was sometimes used as a focal point for discussion; members then prepared and shared foods associated with the chosen region. When the subject was Cuba, for example, members listened to Afro-Cuban jazz, ate rice and beans, smoked Cuban cigars, and discussed *The Mambo Kings Play Songs of Love.*

While a slight alcohol high may add to the vivacity of the group, after the third drink people seem to become peculiarly insistent that their own voice be heard—immediately.

The East Side of Milwaukee Salon, meeting in a beer capital, enjoys imbibing both beer and wine, and have even taken a brewery tour together—but on the whole, nonalcoholic beverages are probably best for discussion's sake. While a slight high may add to the vivacity and conviviality of the group, overindulgence may make conversation go flat or become unruly. After the third drink, in particular, people seem to become peculiarly insistent that their own voice be heard, immediately, and sometimes to the detriment of others.

MONEY

Some library associations sponsor salons by providing space, use of a copy machine, and information. Issue-oriented study circles are sometimes funded through foundations or government agencies. But most salons are self-supporting. The chief salon expenses are generally for refreshments and postage for notices or newsletters. Refreshment costs can be shared by asking everyone to bring food, as in a potluck, while postage costs will most likely be covered if each person contributes a dollar per meeting. Julius Sokolsky's Manhattan salon charges each member six dollars at each monthly meeting: One dollar goes to cleanup costs, another for postage and mailing, and four dollars to defray the costs of the meal that the salon eats after discussion time is over at 10:00 P.M.

If you are planning a more elaborate project, add up the cost of supplies and divide by the number of people who show up. A few salons ask for five- or ten-dollar donations at each meeting, saving the money to finance a big annual party or a weekend retreat, or to hire a lecturer. But remember that salons are meant to be free, or nearly so. If there are expensive dues, someone is running a business and calling it a salon.

IF YOU HAVE TROUBLE . . .

If the discussion of these matters at your first meeting gets bogged down in contention, you might schedule a second meeting with an experienced salonkeeper as a facilitator and consultant. Some groups have resolved differences by handing out a questionnaire explaining various options, then tabulating responses and discussing them at a second planning meeting. A playful group could draw suggestions from a hat or roll dice to choose between different possibilities.

As a final alternative, you can decide to settle on one salon format temporarily. Follow up by holding an organizational meeting after three to six salon sessions, to decide whether you need to change anything. Here is a "template" that works well:

- Hold a basic conversational salon, choosing one topic for each meeting.
- Choose one weekday evening per month (the first Tuesday of each month, for example), and plan on meeting for about two hours. Stick to the same day and time.
- Meet at the same person's home each time. Ideally, it should be centrally located and offer a room large enough to seat fifteen people in reasonable comfort.
- Choose a topic for the first salon by brainstorming a list of subjects, then voting. Allow people to vote for as many topics as they like. When you've isolated one that everyone is interested in, you've found your topic.
- Choose someone to make and send notices of the place, time, and topic of the first salon meeting. This person can also act as facilitator for the initial session. At the end of each meeting, ask for a volunteer to send the next notice and facilitate the next salon.
- Collect one dollar per person, and give the proceeds to the person who is handling the mailing.
- Bring potluck snacks and beverages, but don't plan any major meals.
- Encourage people to invite friends. Add them to your mailing list.

THE RULE OF THREE

Whatever format and practices you initially adopt, give your salon at least three sessions before you make significant changes. People need to become comfortable with a process before they can make good use of it.

Even the most exciting salons flop occasionally, so one dull evening in your new salon doesn't mean that you should toss out the whole structure. The Rule of Three gives people a chance to gain perspective, to relax, to experience the salon as participants rather than critics. After three or more sessions, you can meet specifically to discuss what has been working and consider whether changes might benefit the salon.

In everything your salon attempts, trust your own inclinations. Many exciting, vital salons contradict everything that's been written here. These salons work because they evolved directly out of the values, commitment, and imagination of the people who created them. "I would like to stress the importance of a salon finding its own voice," says Richard Rogers, a Washington State salonist. "Guidelines and suggestions will be valuable, but every group of people has unique wants and needs. Respect them, and the salon will work for you."

CHAPTER FOUR

THE SALON SITE:

CHOOSING A MEETING PLACE

I have always known how to make rooms that have power in them.
    ~ Mabel Dodge

In careful preparation for the salon she intended to hold—and triumph with—in 1913, Mabel Dodge practically gutted her house at 23 Fifth Avenue, painted all her woodwork white, covered the walls with white paper, and then added a chandelier and porcelain roses with stuffed birds perching among them. In ingenuity and sheer will-to-salon power, she belongs with the great women of the tradition.

Which is not to say that you have to refit your own living room in order to hold a successful salon. But the choice and cultivation of venue can do much to ensure your salon's success.

THE IN-HOME SALON

Salons were named after the room in which they were held—*salon* originally meant a high-ceilinged formal reception room in a palace, then a smaller receiving room in an aristocratic house. Meeting in a private home can reinforce your salon's distinctive identity as well as continue a tradition. A room that is familiar, comfortable, and influenced by the people who live there encourages intimacy and informality. Unlike Mabel Dodge, few of us can afford to reserve one room exclusively for conversation, and there's certainly no obligation to replicate this ideal situation. What matters most is comfort and a personal setting. Don't obsess about tidiness: "A hostess should never apologize for any failure in her household arrangements," said Gertrude Stein. One Vermont salon meets in members' homes because, as a member puts it, "we like to relax, to lie on the floor if we feel like it. Our host is whoever thinks they can clean up their place in time."

Besides, artifacts of past salons—doodles and poems taped to the refrigerator, swapped books and photocopied articles left on coffee tables, flyers advertising previous meetings—signify shared experiences.

They're evidence that a community is developing. They imbue your salon with a sense of place.

Some people hesitate to host a salon in a smallish house or apartment because they feel there won't be enough space. This wasn't a hesitation that the grand salonists shared. Both Madame du Deffand and her protégée/nemesis Julie de Lespinasse received in decidedly modest-sized rooms. And why not? Many people feel lost or insignificant in a large room. Physical proximity can create a friendly and informal environment that helps people open up. The ideal is just enough space for everyone, so the arrival of a few latecomers provides an opportunity for some amiable squeezing-together.

The ideal is just enough space for everyone, so the arrival of a few latecomers provides an opportunity for some amiable squeezing-together.

The downside of close quarters? Somebody who feels that his or her personal space has been violated may become argumentative. Introverts, hesitant to offend people who are sitting inches away, might fall silent. If you stay alert to these potential difficulties, offering anyone who appears uncomfortable repeated assurances that they are welcome, your salon members will soon feel at ease with one another.

It's a good idea to use light to create drama in a salon space. Try for a variety of light sources and directions. Areas of shadow allow people to retreat and relax, while the brighter areas help them see and focus on each other. Pools of warm light create "stage" spaces that dramatize and vivify. The best lights are those that soothe with their warmth: sunlight, firelight, and low-watt incandescent bulbs. If only the chilly blue of fluorescents is available, compensate with furnishings (rugs, slipcovers, wall hangings) in warm browns, reds, yellow-toned greens, or grays.

The placement of furniture can serve much the same function as light, drawing attention to certain parts of the room and allowing some people to listen comfortably while others speak. The friendliest and most egalitarian seating arrangement is a circle. In a small circle, all participants can see each other, no two people are so far apart that they can't easily talk with one another, and no one is in a "power spot" for dominating the conversation. A rough amoeba of chairs, pillows, and couches seems to work better than a Platonically perfect circle. Asymmetry allows people to choose the spot in the room that best matches their mood. Introverts or newcomers may choose a chair farther from the center, while extroverts and old-timers may crowd together on a couch. You can place one side against a wall, but be sure to leave plenty of room to move around the remaining perimeter. Let your members rearrange the sofas, chairs, and cushions as they see fit, so they can face different people as the evening progresses.

By all means shift the furniture around from time to time, to break habitual seating patterns and "territories." The change may stimulate new perspectives and interactions. Members who have rarely spoken may suddenly feel encouraged to hold forth, without knowing exactly why. Gertrude Stein was a master of powerful seating arrangements. On one of her artist-filled evenings, she placed each arriving painter in a chair opposite one of his own paintings. "They were so happy that we had to send out twice for more bread," she reported. "Nobody noticed my little arrangement except Matisse, and he did not until just as he left, and now he says it is a proof that I am very wicked."

Gertrude Stein's digs at 27 rue de Fleurus, Paris

Whatever the arrangements, meeting at a consistent location is important. It allows members to find their way to the salon month after month, and those who have been absent for a while can return with ease. A regular meeting place also helps people relax—they know which cupboard holds the glasses and where to find the bathroom.

This doesn't mean you can't change the location occasionally, especially if you're meeting in a home. Your members may enjoy variety, your customary host may need a break, or you may wish to emphasize that the regular host is not the "leader" of the salon. Salons in remote areas, which may draw members from many miles apart, sometimes rotate so that members can take turns driving long distances. In any event, rotating the meeting place works best with a close-knit group of people who feel comfortable in any member's home, and it brings with it practical requirements: You need to keep everyone informed about the locations, provide directions, and coordinate transportation.

PUBLIC SPACES

Public places such as cafés, coffeehouses, and libraries have also played a colorful role in the history of salons. We needn't look further than the Pombo, the Madrid café where Ramón Gómez de la Serna held forth in the 1920s and 1930s (the tertulianos called its basement, where they met, the "Sacred Crypt"). The Rose Room of the Algonquin Hotel in Manhattan was home away from home for the Algonquin Round Table.

The buzz of public life around these salons added something special to them: a flair and a risk-taking energy. The open, freely mixing ambience of a public meeting place can also add a steady stream of newcomers with new ideas. Public places may appeal to contemporary salonists for safety reasons, or simply because no one wants to host. As a bonus, public places are more likely to be wheelchair accessible and easy to reach via public transport. Community centers, libraries, and churches may offer child-care facilities or a playroom for salonists' children.

Some salons go well beyond these limits. In an Amsterdam hotel called De Filosoof, each room is decorated in a theme that recalls a different philosopher, with quotes from the thinker in question displayed on the wall. Members of the Association of Practical Philosophy—teachers, writers, business managers, journalists—meet each month in the hotel's cozy salon to smoke cigarettes, drink martinis and *jenever* (Dutch gin), and discuss the meaning of life. They share a desire to apply abstract philosophy to everyday situations. Municipal officials from six major cities in Holland have asked these practical philosophers for help in solving a whole range of social problems.

Even salons can hold salons. Beauty parlors and barbershops have been traditionally splendid sites for community conversation. Updating this tradition, Minneapolis beauty parlor owner Lynn Baskerfield held monthly gatherings after business hours to discuss a wide range of topics, publicizing the salon-salons in her salon newsletter, *The Conscious Body*. (She set up meditative retreats for her customers, too, and donated 5 percent of the income from her business to peace, justice, and environmental groups.)

Be warned, however: Few public places were designed for conversation. Libraries are built to encourage silence; coffee shop owners may purposely install uncomfortable seats to ensure rapid turnover; cafés may play loud music or offer bright, echoing rooms in which conversation becomes cacophony. Noisy laughter, beverages, or messy art supplies may be verboten, and hours inflexible. "We found ourselves continuing the conversation in the parking lot after the library closed at nine o'clock," lamented Dallas–Fort Worth salonist Mike McCauley. "It was funny for a while, but it got to be an irritant." One salon in the Dallas–Fort Worth area stopped meeting at the local library, in part because the vinyl-covered folding chairs and steel tables were so unattractive. When the salon began meeting at a member's home, the group relaxed and conversation became more open.

ROBERT DE MICHIELL

Other potential problems are availability and cost, as Louise Davida discovered while searching for a meeting place for her Westport, Connecticut, salon. She tried the public library first. There was a space, but it wasn't available until after Labor Day. She found that the YMCA charged $30 an hour, and even churches and synagogues wanted steep "rent." A restaurant will probably expect your group to order food and drink, a process that interrupts the flow of conversation. For all of these reasons, visit and examine your potential public salon space before committing to it.

CAFÉS AND COFFEEHOUSES

"The Turks called coffeehouses 'schools of the wise,'" says San Francisco café salonist Camille M. Stupar. "In Britain they were known as 'penny universities.' Cafés have always been centers of intellectual and artistic activity, birthplaces of new ideas, foundries of revolution." Reason enough to consider them for your own salon—not to mention the matter of convenience. The coffeehouse or café salon is the most natural outgrowth of the living room salon. Meeting in a café requires little planning or organizing. Food and drink are readily available, which may encourage longer talks. People come and go as they please, without invitation or the need to make an extended commitment. Because they are completely available to the public, these groups can be the most egalitarian of salons. And holding a gathering in a café is certainly a good way to make your group visible to the local community.

> **C**afés have always been centers of intellectual and artistic activity, birthplaces of new ideas, foundries of revolution.

If you want to convene regularly in a café, notify management ahead of time and get consent. Find out what the least busy hours are, whether it will be all right if some people don't order refreshments, and whether you can move tables and chairs around to accommodate a crowd of a dozen or more. Some owners discourage lingering, but many others recognize that encouraging a regular clientele is good for business, and that salonists are likely to return to the café when they're not saloning and to recommend it to friends. If the space is appropriate, you might suggest that the café owner set aside one large, round table for general conversation. This is common in Germany, where every local tavern and café has its *Stammtisch,* or "root table," reserved for groups who get together regularly.

Salonkeeper Erika Sukstorf was remarkably successful in starting what she called "guerrilla coffeehouse salons" in Los Angeles. She visited neighborhood cafés, asking the owners if she could designate certain nights of the week as salon nights. She then posted flyers explaining which night a discussion would be held in each coffeehouse, defining each salon as "a gathering of individuals who chew on topics of their choice." Sukstorf was present to get each of the first discussions started, and then the salons took off without her, generating more salons in other cafés. She found that people who initially wanted little more than to get out of their houses soon became very involved. "Every salon has a different character to it," Sukstorf explains. "Coffeehouses are brilliant that way— very open, always changing, always new people."

Sometimes a salon can turn the café into a booming business. This happened to the White Dog Cafe in Philadelphia, which metamorphosed from a small muffin shop into a well-known restaurant, thanks in good part to the café's Table Talks. Proprietor Judy Wicks began by hosting lectures at her café. The lectures now accompany Monday-night dinners and weekend brunches. Topics have included

Judy Wicks, founder of the White Dog Café

the role of universities in American cities, conspiracy theories, the importance of humor in healing physical illness, and "The Struggle for the Soul of the Republican Party," to name just a few.

A great deal grew out of the lectures. A Table Talk session sparked the Philadelphia Swing Project, which raised money to supply swings for children's playgrounds. Wicks went on to encourage her customers to eat in "sister" restaurants in African American, Latino, and Korean neighborhoods. White Dog Cafe employees worked with West Philadelphia High School students as mentors, and the restaurant awarded a culinary scholarship to a graduating high school student each year.

In the "Table for Five Billion, Please!" project, Wicks led diners on visits to countries that are diplomatically distant from the United States. The person-to-person diplomats ate in "sister" restaurants in each country. "We call it 'eating with the enemy,'" says Wicks. And in November 1999, the café sponsored a tour of successful inner-city business and community development projects—with breakfast and lunch at the White Dog. These local and international activities garnered acclaim—and a highly supportive patronage for the restaurant.

BOOKSTORES

Many bookstores host author readings followed by question-and-answer periods. Some stores invite local writers to sit in a circle with store patrons and discuss a topic chosen for the evening. Others dispense with the author focus altogether and simply make their space available to community members for regular discussions. This sort of gathering is identical to a salon.

Glenda Martin and Mollie Hoben founded the *Minnesota Women's Press* newspaper in the Twin Cities in 1985. Two years later they began to hold book groups in which women could read and discuss women's writing. The book groups continue to this day, in the *MWP* bookstore in St. Paul. By encouraging people to seek out a variety of views and

COURTESY OF WASHINGTON AREA ARTISTS' SALON

The Washington Area Artists' Salon shares space with an ethnic arts group at a bookstore in Alexandria, Virginia

opinions on selected topics, Martin conducts her book groups much like salons. (See chapter 10 for more on bookstores and book groups.)

As with any potential meeting place, visit a bookstore you're considering to ensure that it's suitable. Noise and jostling can be a problem in some large bookstores. Smaller ones may simply lack the space to accommodate your salon.

LIBRARIES

Salons and books also come together naturally in libraries, safe public places that often attract a diverse crowd. Dorothy Puryear, a special services librarian, and Ron Gross, a freelance editor, have been hosting successful monthly Roundtables at branch libraries in Long Island for more than a decade. "The participants are, quite simply, whoever wants to come," Gross has written. "A core of 'regulars' soon emerges at each site, but newcomers turn up constantly, drawn by the special attraction of an evening's topic."

Libraries work best for groups that prefer a studious, more or less formal approach to discussion. They offer resources that no single person has at his or her fingertips, and easy access to books and databases can broaden the discussion. Librarians and volunteers are frequently willing to sponsor the group, and they may also lend their time and office facilities to your efforts to publicize your salon.

Find out beforehand if it's appropriate to bring snacks and beverages into the library, and be certain that the library will allow you to make a little noise as your discussions heat up. You may need to book the space several months in advance, and if you meet in the evening you may be required to quit relatively early. (Experienced library salonists suggest that it's good diplomacy to approach the head librarian before going to the library board, ensuring the goodwill of the person who is, after all, on the spot.)

SEMIPUBLIC MEETING PLACES

Semipublic places include conference rooms in business centers (often available at night for employees); common or party rooms in condominiums and big apartment buildings (for use by residents); studios, galleries, and back rooms of small businesses and nonprofit organizations.

Obviously, you need an inside contact to gain access to them. Semi-public places combine some of the advantages of a home with some of those offered by public meeting places. They are often free and relatively private, yet roomier and more accessible than many apartments. On the other hand, they usually lack personality. They can be more severely afflicted with molded-plastic-chair syndrome than the tackiest public space. They're best for a salon that's nervous about meeting in someone's home but wants to ensure a closed membership.

BUSINESS SPACES

Private or semiprivate business sites—retreat centers, conference halls, and hotels—can provide excellent, quiet meeting rooms. A number of corporations have allowed salons to meet in their conference facilities after hours, based on employees' requests. Yet, from the salonists' perspective, there are some potential disadvantages to consider. Employees of the company that's providing the space may be reluctant to return to their workplace in the evening for an after-hours salon. If all the salon members are drawn from the corporate culture, "groupthink" and homogeneity of experience and opinion may be a problem. And if the salon is officially sponsored by an employer, employees may hesitate to speak openly, for fear of future consequences. It goes without saying that a salon on corporate premises needs to be a true salon: If profit, training, or propaganda are the primary goals, it will probably fail.

The news and entertainment industries have sponsored a number of salons in recent years. Sponsorship offers magazines, newspapers, and radio and television stations new avenues of communication with their publics. For the salonists, the big advantage usually is that the communications company will publicize the group's opinions, suggestions, and activities in one way or another. This is particularly useful for salons that are addressing community and social problems. Salon members may be asked to fill out ballots or questionnaires at the end of their discussions—a situation that can work for or against the salon. On the one hand, members may enjoy seeing their discussions and responses used as a basis for subsequent articles or news reports. On the other hand, the ballots or questionnaires may be constructed in a biased or simplistic manner, limiting the salon members' ability to supply meaningful feedback. If you're participating in a sponsored salon, make sure that all the materials provided by your sponsors are fair, objective, and comprehensive. The emphasis should remain on free and open consideration of all alternatives within the specified topics—the irreducible essence of the salon experience.

MEETING OUTDOORS

When Plum Johnson of Toronto was vacationing on a beach in Antigua, a salon mood came over her and she approached other vacationers around the hotel pool and asked if they wanted to participate in a discussion. Agreeing, they dragged their lounge chairs into the shallows of the sparkling blue ocean. "Using the six *Utne Readers* I had brought down in my suitcase for just such an experiment, [we] got to know each other," she reported. "The truth of the matter is that most vacationers are starved for reading material in places like this after about the fifth day. They're also extremely malleable. Their defenses are down. Sun, surf, and rum punches do that."

The great outdoors is (usually) free salon space, and may be exhilarating. The biggest problem associated with it is noise, particularly in urban settings; after all, most public parks are lined on all sides by whizzing traffic. Changes in the weather, the possibility of insect attacks, and staring passersby can also make your salon idyll more trying than you might expect.

CHAPTER FIVE

FINDING PEOPLE:

BUILDING YOUR MEMBERSHIP

Give me new faces, new faces.
   ~ Gertrude Stein

There's a contemporary engraving of Madame Geoffrin's eighteenth-century salon that shows no fewer than fifty bewigged worthies forming a three-tiered circle in Madame's sitting room. Other salon views of the era show a mere ten or twelve salonists in conversation. The charming Madame de Boufflers' fashionable and musical, if not intellectually outstanding, mid-eighteenth-century salon was regularly jammed with a hundred and fifty people—all standing, of course, and content with the merest smile from their vivacious hostess. Indeed, there's no hard-and-fast rule about salon size, but experience suggests sticking to the low end—the best conversations happen in a group of eight to twelve people.

There are several reasons for setting an approximate limit on how many people participate in your salon. The primary one is that the more people there are, the less likely it is that everyone will talk. Anthropologist Bernard Bass has found that, on average, one person in a group of twelve remains silent. In a group of twenty-four people, six of them will clam up. This is due mainly to physical constraints—the more people you add to a circle, the larger it becomes and the harder everyone has to strain to hear. Those with quiet voices or retiring personalities may give up the fight to make themselves heard.

In addition, the more people there are, the more complex their interrelationships become. It gets harder to remember names and make personal contact with everyone. It also becomes difficult to stay flexible enough so that everyone has an equal say in how the group operates. If your group values egalitarian involvement, establishing community, and encouraging friendships, a larger group probably won't work for you.

As with any other rule, there are exceptions to these size principles. A task-oriented group such as a study circle can function well with as few as five people. At the other end of the scale, there are successful salons with from thirty to ninety. (The goal of size here is to garner as many perspectives and opinions as possible.) Usually, though, these large groups break into much smaller groups for the purposes of conversation.

A salon in East San Diego, California, experienced a sudden explosion in membership following media coverage. Rather than trying to limit the number of participants, the group began breaking into small subgroups two or three times during each session, shuffling the people each time and discussing whatever subjects came up. Each half hour, the group reassembled and counted off by fives. After doing this for several meetings, the salonists were familiar enough with each other that they could have open and productive discussions in the full circle without subgrouping as often. If a number of new members show up on a particular night, the salon returns to the get-acquainted subgrouping for a while.

A long-running salon in San Francisco called A New American Place often attracts as many as eighty participants. At a typical meeting, members see a short presentation, break into small groups for about forty-five minutes, then reconvene with all members for general conversation.

Some groups have found that a closed membership is crucial for establishing intimacy and trust. Washington salonist Richard Rogers recalled that members of his salon began talking about the need for "new blood" about a year after the salon was formed. "We had reached a level of comfort and wanted to add new members to create a fresh outlook," he explained. Ultimately, though, they decided to wait. After a time, they discovered that the original members were able to take the conversation deeper and rekindle their spirits. In Julius Sokolsky's long-running and very cohesive Manhattan salon, they've reached the limit that can be accommodated in any of the members' apartments, and choose not to meet in public.

Whatever size you decide your salon should be, be aware that between one-fifth and one-third of those on an invitation list will actually materialize. If almost everyone has expressed emphatic interest, the one-third estimate applies. If your group is just starting, the topic is obscure, or you are meeting near holidays, apply the one-fifth estimate. Your total membership pool should be at least three times as large as the number of people you hope to attract. If you want the "ideal" eight to twelve, an overall membership pool of twenty-four to thirty-six people should produce the right number on any given night. A creativity salon with twenty to thirty participants at every meeting might maintain a membership list of sixty to one hundred.

INVITATIONS

How you invite people to your salon and the methods you use for keeping in touch can serve either to expand or to limit the number of people who are present at any given meeting.

Informal verbal invitations to friends and casual acquaintances can be very productive. Salonist Susan M. Neulist-Coelho drew her salon members from women who regularly patronized her espresso stand in Rogue River, Oregon. One California salonist started by inviting everyone he met for a period of time. The result, as you might expect, was an extraordinary combination of people: members of the South Bay chapter of American Atheists; lesbian prostitutes he met at a picnic; and a number of current and former clergymen from his religious community. The amazingly diverse Washington Area Artists' Salon, which runs the gamut from unemployed poets to psychologists, has talked about everything from "the business of art" to "creativity and clutter."

> One salonist started by inviting everyone he met for a period of time. The result was an extraordinary combination of people: members of American Atheists, lesbian prostitutes, and clergymen.

If your salon is being organized by a small group of people, the simplest approach is asking each member of the core group to invite five people to the first salon meeting. At that meeting, ask everyone who attends to bring their friends, roommates, out-of-town guests, and interested acquaintances to the next one. This method produces new faces without losing a feeling of connectedness, and interested newcomers can be added to a mailing or phone list so they'll be aware of future meetings. You can reinforce your verbal invitations by handing out calling cards that specify the name of the salon, the meeting time and place, and the name and phone number of a contact person.

The friends-of-friends method is simple, but it can be a little wearisome: You have to "sell" the salon idea to people who don't know anything about it. You may meet resistance to the method from members who want to salon beyond the boundaries of their social circle. Still others may be concerned that factions will develop if salon members bring personal friends. If you share these concerns, if you live in an area where you don't know anybody, or if your salon is suffering from membership attrition, you may prefer to recruit through a membership list.

ADVERTISING

Membership lists and networking through acquaintances are convenient, but they reach a relatively narrow spectrum of people. If you want to widen the circle, try advertising for salon members. Jaime Guerrero of Philadelphia started his salon with a mass mailing to names on a salon list, but only five people showed up consistently. The core members decided to conduct a poster recruiting campaign. They posted announcements at the places they frequented, including markets, cafés, repertoire movie theaters, restaurants, performance spaces, record shops, and college campuses. An announcement at a popular bookstore elicited the biggest response. The group's membership list eventually swelled to around sixty people, although—and this is typical—only twelve to fifteen of them turned up at any given meeting.

If you decide to hand out flyers or put up posters, make them brief and easy to read. Graphics should be bold and simple. A vague, wordy announcement that asks for donations or solicits potluck contributions is unlikely to garner much response. If you meet in a public setting, list where and when you meet. If you meet in someone's home, it's best to give a contact name and number so you can screen prospective members on the phone. Some salons have successfully advertised in local newspapers or posted announcements on local computer bulletin boards. Like postering, this kind of advertising attracts a diverse membership and is easy to discontinue once you've reached your ideal size.

If you have a stable membership, you may want to recruit new members only occasionally. You might do this by attending regional salon gatherings (described in a later chapter) or by conducting an annual membership drive. Ron Gross described the procedure that works for the Nassau, New York, library salons he's involved with:

> Once or twice a year, the groups throw an open house, which is widely publicized to the community by the library, via its newsletter, flyers, posters, a story in the local paper, and so on. Some topic of wide interest is presented, or a compelling guest speaker. . . . Attendees at these open houses can sign up to receive notices of the next few meetings of the group, and some become regular members.

This kind of short-lived membership drive is a good way to stir up interest in your salon without having to deal with inquiries from strangers throughout the year.

Once you've established a membership base, you'll need to decide how best to stay in touch with everyone.

Phone trees are an excellent way to keep the salon message going out. One person calls four or five other people—the first branching of the tree. Each of these people in turn has a list of four or five additional people to call, and so on to the end of the membership list. The first caller is generally the coordinator, in charge of tracking all phone numbers, determining who is responsible for calling whom, and assigning new members to callers. Callers who will be out of town notify the coordinator, who ensures that someone else makes their calls. Calls should be brief and simple: the time and place of the salon and the activity or topic scheduled for the meeting.

It's best to make reminder calls three or four days before the session—not so early that members might forget the meeting, nor so close to the date that they may have made other plans.

You can "prune" a phone tree that's grown too large by asking everyone who is called to contact the coordinator and confirm that they would like to remain on the list. You'll find that some people who only make it to the salon once a year are nevertheless enthusiastic about getting their monthly calls.

Some salons use postcards and postcard trees, which work just as well as long as you need to convey only a short, simple reminder. If your salon rotates homes or meets irregularly, if you need to provide maps, or if you want to include short readings with your topic announcements, you'll probably be better served by a one-page flyer or a newsletter.

The salonists of the classic tradition kept their pens perpetually at hand for jotting down memorable phrases, tidbits of gossip, and sudden news flashes that they could pass on to others in lengthy letters. Their letters served as contemporary commentary on salon society, and as newspapers of a sort for those who were unable to attend a salon. "The talk last night," wrote a discouraged Julie de Lespinasse to a friend, "was like one of those insipid romances at which both reader and author yawn. One has to console oneself as did the King of Prussia on another regrettable occasion [a military defeat], 'We'll do better another time.'"

Many modern salons are equally eager to keep in touch through newsletters. The Arlington Salon in Virginia puts out a newsletter called *Slouching Towards Consensus*, while the Tracy's Tertulia in Minneapolis keeps members and interested friends informed of its doings via the zine-style *Mister Raindrop*. (The group's collective and individual literary efforts also appear, including the Exquisite Corpse collective-writing games that the salon has been enjoying since 1993.) Newsletters often include cartoons, quotes, and short passages from articles on the next salon topic. They may offer recaps of previous discussions and questions for members on how the salon should be run. Newsletters may state the meeting times and places of other salons in the region. They might announce marriages, births, and other life changes in the salon mem-

Salon newsletters from around the country

bership; provide movie and book reviews; and even offer items to swap. When newsletters are circulated among friends, they double as informal advertising for new members.

Newsletters also create continuity between salon gatherings. The Kansas City Public Conversation Salon includes a list of all members and their phone numbers in each newsletter. The names of those who attended the most recent salon are marked, which allows other members to catch up by contacting them. Arlington salonist Ken Schellenberg credits the newsletter with "holding the group together through phases when certain members had classes/volunteer activities that kept them from coming for a few months. For us, the newsletter has been a way to keep the conversation going between meetings."

As delightful as they can be, newsletters are time-consuming, and they can be expensive if they have to be mailed to a large number of people. In some cases, an aspiring writer is happy to be the salon scribe, creating and mailing the newsletter regularly. More often, though, newsletters are reduced to one-page flyers produced by a different person prior to each meeting. In either case, a donation of a dollar or two from those who attend your meeting should cover the costs of copying and mailing.

Deborah Lerme Goodman's Cambridge salon has been thriving since 1991, and she attributes its longevity in part to e-mail. A short group note is sent out one week before the monthly salon meeting to remind members where the salon will be held and what's on the agenda. "I would try to make phone calls to remind people of the meetings," she says, "but didn't always get around to it—or feel like doing it—especially if the salon wasn't meeting at my house."

Should you require members to reply when they're notified of an upcoming meeting? It's usually counterproductive, creating a sense of obligation that's hard on spontaneity. If salonists show up because they're intrigued, not obliged, everyone has more fun, and the salon thrives. Of course, some hosts may feel anxious if they don't know at least approximately how many people will attend a meeting. And if you are planning activities that require materials and preparation, it may be imperative to know how many are coming. A Washington, D.C., salon has solved this problem with a voice mail line; the salon asks everyone who receives the group's flyer to call. If the gathering is getting too big, a message on the voice mail tells late callers that the salon is full and asks them to try again next month.

DIVERSITY

The fundamental thing is not to forget that the salon is a cultural buffet.
~ Mariajose de Calvalho, Brazilian salon muse

Within the obvious limits of era and culture, openness to diversity has been an enduring characteristic of salons. From the aristocratic salons that welcomed the hardworking, freelance-writing philosophes to Mabel Dodge's Park-Avenue-meets-the-underworld milieu, the salon has been open to people on the social, artistic, and intellectual fringe. Modern salonists often start or join a salon because they want to be exposed to new ideas and a broad range of people. And when a salon becomes so comfortable that people no longer disagree with one another, a more diverse membership can relight the spark. Yet one of the most consistent problems that salons face is finding effective ways to add racial, class, and perspectival diversity to groups that are often all liberal, all white, and all economically comfortable. (One Ohio salon had to put a cap on the number of members that were coming from a single Unitarian church.)

Although many modern salons are relatively homogeneous with regard to age and ethnicity, they tend to be quite diverse when it comes to employment. A typical example is the Washington Area Artists' Salon, which despite its name reaches beyond the arts for members. As salonist Daisy Birch explains, the group takes in "poets, jazz musicians, street musicians, dancers, sculptors, choreographers, chefs, scientists, writers, painters, singers, linguists, psychologists, photographers, fashion designers, interior designers, exterior designers, illustrators, classical musicians, humorists, art teachers, accomplished artists, dabbling artists, part-timers, full-timers, unemployed, underemployed, overemployed, etc. There are all kinds, and all are kind."

And while liberal ideas tend to dominate in the salons that have been in touch with *Utne Reader* over the years—causing some conservative members to feel ganged up on—many liberal salons have made good-faith efforts to recruit conservatives and make them feel welcome.

Some groups prefer to limit diversity in some respects while promoting it in others. They want to feel certain that members have enough in common to express themselves freely. Other salons have chosen to maintain a closed membership—not to avoid contact with different perspectives, but because they are trying to create greater intimacy within the existing group. Of course it's important to spend time building a group identity before welcoming strangers into your midst. But in most cases, groups that shut themselves off from other people become more of a club than a community, more of a support group than a salon. They never experience the challenge of encountering a wide range of ideas and experiences, a challenge intrinsic to the salon.

Diversity is easiest to achieve if you strive for it from the start. Begin by considering what diversity means to you, and what kinds of diversity you would like within the group: age, sexual preference, political leanings, religion, ethnic heritage, language, rural versus urban upbringing, class, education, marital status, and so on. If you have decided as a group to welcome diversity, you'll probably find yourselves using the salon-building techniques outlined in this chapter, but casting a wider net. You can extend the personal invitation approach beyond friends to acquaintances and even perfect strangers. Strike up conversations with taxi drivers from the Middle East and Africa, and invite them if you're intrigued by their perspectives. Punks and heavy-metal heads encountered at coffee shops, people you meet while you're apartment hunting, shopping, eating out, and going to parties—all are potential salon members. Assume that everyone you run into could be a fascinating conversationalist—but, of course, spend a little time talking first.

> In most cases, groups that shut themselves off from other people become more of a club than a community, more of a support group than a salon.

If inviting people on the wing seems too risky, visit or advertise in places that reflect the kind of diversity you're looking for: basketball courts, drumming circles, churches, community centers.

Don't forget about retirement homes. Older people often have a great deal of experience with book groups or bridge clubs, and they almost always have fascinating life experiences and opinions to share. Romanian-born Paula Boose wrote to *Utne Reader* hoping to find a salon interested in hearing her voice. She described herself as "seventy years old, a love vegetarian, live around small rural community . . . trouble finding mutually interesting uncommon topics with people. . . . I'm a stranger in the strange land, born by different culture, survivor from World War Two holocaust . . . always I think globally, act vocally." Clearly, a woman who could be an asset to any salon.

Post announcements of your salon in foreign-student centers at the local college or university. Many foreign students and faculty members, especially those who come from cultures where serious discussion and warm face-to-face relationships are the norm, are eager to make personal contact with Americans interested in talking about something more significant than the latest Brad Pitt movie.

If you'd like the input of people who are living in an entirely different social context, try inviting high school students. Their unabashed observations on global and interpersonal issues are often gut-wrenchingly to the point, and many teens are hungry for meaningful talk. In the salon milieu, students may discover caring, trustworthy adult mentors who (to their astonishment) take them seriously.

When you're advertising for new members, be frank about your desire for diversity. Describe your group as a "multicultural salon interested in conversation on a variety of topics that affect all of us," or something similar. Frame your next topic so it interests all kinds of people. For example, if you plan to talk about pollution, entitle your discussion "Pollution Doesn't Recognize National Borders." Consider placing your ad in various newspapers around town, including ethnic ones.

Despite the potential drawbacks, meeting in a public setting is a good way to reach out and be visible to the wider community. (The meeting place should be wheelchair accessible and easy to reach via public transport. If possible, provide a common baby-sitter.) Post notices on the walls of your meeting place, letting other customers or visitors know about the salon and welcoming them to participate.

Whatever method you employ to find people, don't forget to invite newcomers back emphatically and cordially. Ask them if they'd like to be included on your phone tree or mailing list, and encourage them to bring their friends to the next meeting. This will especially help foreign newcomers, who may be shy, uncertain of themselves in your company, and unable to interpret subtler American signals of welcome.

DEALING WITH DIVERSITY

In a letter to *Utne Reader*, Marian and Joe Arminger told the story of their difficult quest for a welcoming, comfortable salon. They described themselves as "staunch Republicans with four children, who are not animal rights activists, who are anti-abortion and anti–population growth control . . . and are anti-homosexual, plus we are also advocates of less government." Rock-ribbed conservatives? Yet the Armingers eat only "organic food, including organic, ethically raised meat, don't wear plastic shoes . . . fight against the use of chemicals as three of our children are chemically sensitive . . . [are] pro–natural childbirth . . . pro-breastfeeding for extended length of time . . . and we're both educated." These interestingly complex people obviously had thought hard about a variety of issues and refused to settle for simplistic or automatic answers. Unfortunately, they dropped out of the first salon they visited. The other members seemed "only interested in like-minded individuals. . . . Obviously, we made the liberals uncomfortable," they wrote. In the end, the Armingers decided to seek a salon composed primarily of other Republicans.

A salon is likely to present just such a wall of homogeneity unless all members actually are willing to entertain challenges to their perspectives and worldviews—which is a different matter from a cozy theoretical diversity. If your group is lucky enough to be drawing members from different cultural backgrounds, you will probably encounter a variety of communication styles, norms for physical and emotional closeness, educational backgrounds, ethical systems, and perhaps languages. To handle these differences, everyone needs to be tactful, curious about one another, and frank about themselves.

The first principle: No tokenism. No Democrat should be expected to speak for all Democrats, no African American for all people of color, no Catholic for all Christians, no high school student for all teenagers. Turning salonists into "spokespeople" or "experts" sets them apart from other members and may intimidate the rest of the group, too. A powerful antidote to tokenism is exploring the individual histories of all the salon members. Take the time to find out about one another's backgrounds, ages, economic situations, studies, hobbies, jobs, travels, aspirations, politics, and religious beliefs. When all members have revealed a good deal about their personal backgrounds, it will be nearly impossible to see anybody as the representative of a demographic group.

A shortcut to self-revelation is the question-and-answer game called Two Truths, One Lie. Ask all your members to come prepared to make two true statements and one false one about themselves. (All three statements should refer to things no one else would know about them.) As each person speaks, the others try to sift truth from falsehood. The speaker then reveals the truth. Two Truths, One Lie not only provides information; it reveals the assumptions we make about one another in a particularly clear (and funny) light. You can encourage greater mutual understanding by putting personal questions on the salon agenda or adopting the council method of discussion, in which each person speaks in turn without interruption.

If people from varying backgrounds are not returning or inviting their friends to your salon, maybe the behavior you expect is too rigid. People from non-Western cultures may be more comfortable arguing loudly or exchanging affectionate insults than other salon members—or they may be more restrained. Expand or alter your norms as you see fit, but let newcomers know your ground rules and expectations—it's another way of making them welcome.

If some salonists don't speak standard American English as their first or primary language, the rest of the group may need to speak more slowly and clearly, and to offer clarification at important junctures. (Those guests also have a responsibility to ask for clarification if they're having trouble understanding, as do English-speaking visitors to salons conducted in other languages.) Don't let this process bog down the rhythm of your conversations—limit your explanations to key points and obscure jokes. Constantly focusing on the nonnative speaker will cause more embarrassment than enlightenment.

As you discover cultural subjects about which most of the group is ignorant, take the time to educate yourselves. Ask the most knowledgeable person in the group for suggested readings or topic ideas. For a time, you might turn your salon into a book club or study circle, reading and discussing key texts on immigration movements, slavery, feminism, colonialism, world religions, non-Western history, or whatever other topic has emerged. Read a range of foreign novels, visit museums and unfamiliar places of worship, or contact cultural centers to learn about upcoming events.

Some salons have asked foreign scholars and other visitors to give lectures on their religion or heritage, then answer questions from salon members. During the Gulf War, for example, several salons invited Middle Eastern Muslims to provide a perspective on the conflict and the cultures involved. The salonists reported that they gained greater respect for a religion and a part of the world they had known little about. Not that you have to go outside of the country's borders to encounter a "foreign" culture. The Cincinnati RADS salon has hosted an Amish couple from just down the road, who described their lives and answered questions. (Remember, though, that even a very knowledgeable guest can't be expected to speak for all members of a culture, heritage, or system of beliefs.)

Finally, don't forget to celebrate your diversity. You might stage an annual "family tree" meeting, at which participants bring food, play music, show artifacts, and wear clothes that represent an ethnic branch on their family tree or a country they've lived in for a significant amount of time. The more you explore the diversity within your group, the more you come to accept the uniqueness of each person and value the amazing range of behavior and beliefs that constitutes humanity. This exploration is the essence of the salon.

PART THREE

BIG TALK:
THE ART OF SALON
CONVERSATION

CHAPTER SIX

CHOOSING TOPICS: DECIDING

WHAT TO TALK ABOUT

There are no uninteresting things, there are only uninterested people.
  ~ G.K. Chesterton, English journalist

While any and every kind of subject can spark salon discussion, topics that lend themselves to broad speculation—not simple answers—have the best chance. When the whimsical, iconoclastic former queen of Sweden, Christina, was living in Rome in the latter half of the seventeenth century and holding a notable salon in the beautiful Palazzo Riario, she allowed only the most stimulating of questions to be addressed: Which is better, to deserve or to possess good fortune? Are love and hate the same passion? Which is worse, to deceive or to allow oneself to be deceived? What is the power of love in nature?

In our media-obsessed age, trivial incidents and fads are quickly exhausted unless you can tease out the wider implications of a trend or pop phenomenon. Season your topics, as Christina did, with a soupçon of wit, playfulness, and paradoxicality to keep salon members in a state of fluid curiosity, willing to become engaged, changed, and startled.

Topics should engross, puzzle, challenge, and move your members. When your group is brainstorming topics, note those that change the mood of the room—ideas that people start talking about immediately, too fascinated to wait for the next salon. Interrogate any topic that comes with a "should" attached (as in "We really *should* address global warming") to see if your salonists truly are keen on it. Salons arise from the need to make sense of the world. Trust that what feels important to your members really is.

> Salons arise from the need to make sense of the world. Trust that what feels important to your members really is.

Face even the most controversial and most scholarly topics fearlessly—you'll be keeping faith with the salon tradition, in which the finest minds of Europe presented their most challenging work and speculations to salon audiences. Descartes' *Discourse on Method*, the Magna Carta of modern science, was worked out in Madame de Rambouillet's seventeenth-century salon—not to mention the world-changing ideas that the philosophes aired *chez* Julie de Lespinasse and Madame Geoffrin a century later.

No Descartes in your group? Don't worry. Almost any subject—first encounters with racism, defining ethics in a secular society, theories of brain functions, the implications of bioengineered foods—can be thought out and presented in an accessible way. Modern salon groups such as the Mind Spa, which meets in the Nassau County Library in New Jersey, have vigorously discussed biofeedback, the causes of suicide, the origin of zero in mathematics, and four kinds of luck. Daria Stermac's very cosmopolitan Toronto salon has boldly gone into global economics, theater as social activism, near-death experiences, and nothing less than "Reconstructing the Human Race." Translating difficult topics into everyday language and believing that each of us has the necessary wisdom to form conclusions are fundamental aspects of the salon.

If someone in the group suggests an intriguing topic that other members don't know much about, ask the suggester to provide a short written synopsis or a ten-minute verbal presentation at the next meeting, addressing the challenging subject in straightforward language. Then, with everyone at least slightly oriented, begin the discussion. Once your group understands the fundamentals of the topic, members can draw upon their general knowledge and personal experiences to discuss its implications. If they feel the need for more in-depth information, you can form a study circle and explore the topic for a number of meetings. You might invite guest speakers or choose relevant readings.

Most salons try to strike a balance between so-called "hard" subjects (mathematics, the sciences, technology, politics, economics) and "soft" ones (philosophy, human relationships, social science, arts, and culture). Whether the subject is hard or soft, discussion can range from the anecdotal to the scholarly, depending on the mood of the group and the way the topic is presented. Minneapolis salonist Judy Bell considers variety the most important thing in choosing topics. The café salon she attends mixes the political and the cultural with, as she puts it, "topics you'll think about in conjunction with your work or your whole life." The salon spices its list of subjects—personal well-being, food, the environment, health care—with unconventional topics like "The Reptilian Mind" and "Non-Ordinary Reality."

Oh, and don't forget sheer frivolity. "We did not talk so much of politics," said a guest at Rahel Levin's nineteenth-century Berlin salon, "as of Parisian manners, pleasures and wickedness, of love affairs, theaters, restaurants—all delightful subjects, are they not?" Serious-minded salons often set aside time for pure gossip and other social banter at the beginning of the evening. If your salon has been digging deeply into heavy topics for quite a while, you might schedule an entire session of unapologetic Levin-style frivolity as a change of pace. Fashion (in clothing, cars, computers, etc.), favorite restaurants, films, TV series, and other aspects of the passing parade are fair game. Games of all sorts (see the section on creativity salons in chapter 9) can also lighten things up.

HOW TO CHOOSE TOPICS

"Our topics are always decided by consensus," says salonist Ken Schellenberg. "We toss around some ideas and just keep brainstorming until we get a majority of heads nodding in agreement." Topic selection may work just that easily for your group, or you may need a bit more structure. The simplest way to start deciding what to talk about is to brainstorm a list of potential topics at your first organizational meeting (as sketched in chapter 3). Ask the open-ended question "What topics would you like to talk about in the salon?" and establish a time limit (fifteen minutes is good). During that period the salonists should feel comfortable saying anything that comes to mind—without hesitation, without expecting a response, and without defending or explaining their suggestions. During brainstorming, no judgment, positive or negative, is expressed—not even a shake or nod of the head. If people run out of ideas before the time limit is up, repeat the question or pose it differently: "What subjects keep coming up with you and your friends?" "What's been occupying your mind lately?"

Have someone write down all the topic suggestions. The "scribe" may also make suggestions, but he or she has to say them out loud before writing them down. If two people take notes, you're likely to harvest more ideas—one will catch what the other misses. Some groups record all the suggestions on a big sheet of paper at the front of the room, although this can distract the brainstormers.

When time is up, or when the flow of ideas peters out, the scribe reads back all suggestions, again without discussion. Rephrase suggestions if the people who forwarded them feel the scribe didn't capture their intent. Finally, read the list once again, this time with some discussion of the suggestions. Which ones make you think? Are you eager to talk about a given topic immediately? Is it something you haven't thought much about and want to explore? Allow people to vote for as many topics as they like, then tally the votes and rank the topics. In most cases, two or three will emerge as the top contenders. Evaluate these as a group to decide which topic would best launch your first salon, but keep the entire list so you can expand upon it through regular brainstorming and voting sessions at future salons.

A more directed style of brainstorming that helps ensure variety begins with the salon deciding on several broad categories. Put each category—technology, religion, pop culture, relationships, politics, whatever—on a separate piece of paper. After brainstorming for five minutes on each category, you will have five different lists of topics. Vote and rank them as already described, then rotate among the lists each time you meet.

If your group is uncomfortable brainstorming aloud, ask each person to write four or five ideas on a piece of paper. Hold a brief discussion and vote on the list of suggestions. And if voting seems boring, skip it and let the person who has volunteered to facilitate the next salon choose the topic from the brainstormed list—or come up with an entirely different idea. In Judy Bell's salon, volunteer idea-finders are matched with months. "January!" she announces. "Who wants to take it, and what do you want to talk about?" Bell makes a list of dates, facilitators, and topics, then mails it to all members.

Some salons select their topics from lead articles in a magazine that all the members read. Others base discussions on books or films that everyone agrees to read or see beforehand. (You can settle on the films and books by brainstorming.) Bahram Zandi's Cinema Salon in Washington, D.C., is entirely devoted to dining, movie-watching, and discussion of the film afterwards. Salonists convene in a "home theater" in Zandi's basement to watch a foreign or independent film. Zandi and friends began the salon when two beloved revival movie houses in their neighborhood closed their doors.

How often you hold brainstorming sessions is up to the group. A short one at the end of every salon meeting, setting the topic for next time, allows you to respond to interests that may change in the space of a few weeks or months. Deciding every three to six months, or holding a yearly topic-setting potluck party, relieves you of the pressure of making decisions at every meeting.

If your salon has been meeting for some time, is composed of friends with significant common history, or is interested in talking about current events, you may not want or need predetermined topics. Instead, you might start each salon with a round, posing a specific question that stimulates people to reflect on their current concerns: Have you seen anything in the news lately that intrigued or bothered you? What significant events or encounters have happened to you recently? You'll know you've hit the evening's topic when a comment sparks immediate response from the group. Finish the round, take a short break, then return to that winning topic in open discussion. Some groups use these topic rounds at the end of salon meetings in order to garner ideas for the next salon. This can be frustrating, though, if people want to start talking about a subject immediately but have to wait until the next meeting to do so.

> Start each salon with a round, posing a specific question. You'll know you've hit the evening's topic when a comment sparks immediate response from the group.

Or leave the whole question to chance. Ask each person to write one topic suggestion on a piece of paper, put the whole lot in a bag, and draw. You can also roll dice, use a spinner, or otherwise put matters in the hands of fate. Lindsay Dyson of Los Angeles once sent everyone in her salon a small brown paper bag with the following note attached:

> This is a GRAB BAG and so is the next salon so GRAB whatever's been BAGGIN' or BUGGIN' you lately and put it in this BAG and bring it with you. . . . Then whatever is in the BAG will be let out of the BAG and everyone will know what's in your BAG. So maybe it should be something fun or something to eat or something impersonal or political or intellectual but it doesn't have to be, it could be something very intimate that you want everyone to know anyway.
>
> It's up to you. It's your BAG, so fill it up: animal, vegetable, or mineral.
>
> Or maybe yours is mainly an air BAG. It's okay it's your BAG so have fun with/in your BAG.
>
> And we'll see you and your BAG next week. BAGISM lives.

NARROWING TOPICS AND MAKING THEM PERSONAL

If the flow of talk is to get anywhere, if it is to reach a conclusion, it must be confined within a rather narrow channel or it is certain to dissipate itself.

~ Chauncey Brewster Tinker, *The Salon and English Letters*

Suppose you find yourself with a resonant topic that, despite its popularity and importance, just isn't igniting the conversational fires. You may have picked a subject that's simply too broad. Few people can talk about racism, for example, without being intimidated by or getting lost in the sheer enormousness of it. But if you break it down into more specific terms that relate to people's lives, you'll suddenly have a proliferation of topics to choose from, and your conversations are likely to become lively, imaginative, and provocative again.

"I want to forewarn you—tonight's topic seems to be phallocentrism, and Jessica is in a take-no-prisoners mood."

You can narrow the subject by recasting it as a debate or a question with a specific title. The umbrella topic of racism could break down into: "The Rise of Hate Crimes," "Race Prejudice Versus Class Prejudice," "Racism in Schools: Does Integration Work?" "Media Portrayal of Ethnic Minorities," "Ethnic Humor: Caricature or Catharsis?" and so on.

Another route to powerful subjects is to make them personal. Open the salon with a question related to the larger topic: When did you first become aware of racism? How does racism affect you in your daily life? How have you been harmed by racism? Do you think racism is a natural or learned response? Some salons formalize this process by asking a specific personal question in a round, during which no interruption is allowed. Then the topic is opened to general conversation. The initial questions often elicit thoughtful and sensitive responses, building a foundation of trust and honesty that prevails throughout the conversation.

"Why" questions usually lead to philosophical discussions. "How" queries invite practical discussion and problem-solving. The best questions are often those posed spontaneously by salon members. Questions should stimulate, not direct. With the exception of the initial query, they should be derived from the conversation.

It's not only weighty, difficult topics that can benefit from good questions. Judy Bell once started a salon session on solitude by reading a few quotes on the joys of solitude, then explained briefly why the subject has meaning for her. She opened the discussion by posing this question: "Where do you go to be alone?" This highly personal tack defeated generalities and elicited concrete and interesting responses—as well as giving salonists insights into one another's lives. Judy's next question was "What do you do when you're alone?" Once again, personal experiences came pouring out, and the salonists discovered that they did many of the same things in solitude. Then she asked "What things do you reserve only for yourself?" which sent the conversation off in a more philosophical direction. Later, the group discussed related issues, such as how to maintain a sense of independence in a romantic relationship. The conversation rolled on through the evening, never flagging.

Most salons are striving to cover a complex topic in a two- or three-hour session, so some members may feel that digressions are disruptive—and most salons do run smoothly when everyone adheres to the chosen subject. On the other hand, a digression is actually a spontaneously generated new topic, a topic that may grab salonists' attention more forcefully than the original one. You may choose to let digressions take you on new paths, then return to the original topic later in the session or at another one. Letting conversations take their own course can make members more attentive to the flow of talk and energize your salon. Conversations have their own life cycles. Some are brief and bright, while others last many hours over the course of months or years. Any new point of view, discovery, or event can resurrect discussion of an old topic. If your group is willing to return to a subject again and again, each time with deeper insight, you will never run out of things to talk about.

PUTTING TOPICS IN DIFFERENT FRAMEWORKS

Some groups like to debate and compare factual, scientific, and technical information. Others focus mainly on the causes of social problems and brainstorming solutions. Philosophical salons treat questions of ethics and the meaning of life — the favored mode of the historic salons. And others prefer telling stories, with an emphasis on incidents drawn from their personal lives.

The fact is, all salons, whatever their favorite frame of reference, can use all of these approaches at different times — and deliberately change the framework to deepen and broaden the conversation. No matter what you are talking about, you can ask these questions: What are the factual dimensions of the subject? What are its philosophical implications? Are social problems relevant to the subject? What ramifications does the subject have for our personal lives? This multifaceted approach is an excellent way of dealing with emotionally charged or highly complex subjects.

Suppose you've decided to look deeply at racism. You might start with the investigative approach, sharing facts about hate crimes, immigration, genocide, and so on. During this session, read and discuss materials critically, looking for hidden assumptions, errors in experimental setups and conclusions, statistical biases, and social contexts that influence the opinions of the writers.

At your next meeting, shift to a personal approach. In this mode, group members relate incidents of racism they have witnessed or experienced, and explain how they dealt with them.

A session in the philosophical mode might discuss what racism implies about human nature, whether children can be taught to grow up without racist tendencies, or whether racism is a product of nationalism. This sort of conversation can be marvelously creative, as long as the discussion remains open-ended and no one tries to reach definitive conclusions. Baltimore salonist Alan Duckworth not only specializes in philosophical discussion with his group, whose motto is "The Unexamined Discussion May Not Be Worth Having," but also has developed an entire curriculum of philosophical games and discussion formats that any salon can adopt. His "ideatron" and "encephalon" salon formats are recipes for very serious, very focused discussion of what he calls "Class II and III topics," or "ideas, facts, theories"—in contrast to "Class I topics," "the mundane and particular, opinions, beliefs, particulars, the here and now." For Duckworth, "The Rise in Hate Crimes" and "Social Activism on a Tight Schedule" are Class I; Class III might include "What Is Natural and Normal" and "Theories of History."

Or take the social activist approach, brainstorming possible solutions and outcomes. What has and has not worked in the past to solve the racism riddle? What is being done now? What can your members, as a small group or as individuals, hope to accomplish? Tinkering like this in the realm of the possible—even without much hope of a definitive solution—can give your salon a lift.

One of the best reasons to try out different discussion frameworks is that everyone will become more conscious of them as they naturally appear and shift in the course of any conversation. It's natural to jump from facts to assessments to beliefs, or to slip into brainstorming mode—all in the course of a few minutes. Awareness of the modes and their differences will help avoid misunderstanding and confusion—and encourage more precise, conscious contributions from everyone.

If you want to be extra clear on this score, you can use objects to signal which tack you're taking in a discussion. You might keep balls of different colors or other symbolic objects on a table in the center of the room, available for members to hold up as they shift into a particular mode of communication. Picking up a small doll might mean "I'm moving from analysis into storytelling." Holding a rainbow-colored question mark could indicate a switch from fact to speculation. Different people might be assigned to tackle a question or topic from specific viewpoints, as symbolized by these objects.

Logician Edward de Bono uses "Six Thinking Hats" to represent different thinking modes. The White Hat represents the objective, neutral computer mind, which offers factual information and statistics. The Red Hat stands for the emotional mind, expressing feelings, hunches, intuition. The Black Hat is used for troubleshooting, playing devil's advocate, pointing out risks, and analyzing both past and potential outcomes, while the Yellow Hat represents optimistic thinking, fantasies, opportunities, benefits, and ways of making things work. The Green Hat means fertility, creativity, movement, brainstorming without judging, change, and heading into the unknown; and the Blue Hat is the facilitator's hat, dedicated to process and communications, defining problems, focusing on the agenda at hand, providing overviews and summaries, and asking questions. The wearer of the Blue Hat can suggest to others the hats they might try on.

Try the approach for a session or two. And who's to say six hats are enough? You could add a Purple Hat to indicate mystical, spiritual, or dreamlike communication, a Dark Red Hat to represent physical reactions and instincts, or a Rainbow Hat to represent the multicultural or global view. Even if you don't use the hats all the time, they can serve as visible reminders of the many directions your discussion can take.

CHAPTER SEVEN

SPEECH AND SILENCE: THE ART OF SUCCESSFUL CONVERSATION

You go to see each other; you talk about the good weather and the bad; everyone says, unaffectedly, what passes through his head; some are grave, others extravagant; some are old, and others are young; some are profound, and several are innocent. Madame asks a malicious question; Monsieur makes a biting answer. An enthusiast eagerly tells a story, a frondeur makes a harsh criticism; a gossip interrupts the conversation, an epigram wakes it up, a passionate tribute sets it afire . . . a wild joke brings it to an end, and puts everyone into agreement. Time passes, people separate; everyone is happy, everyone has had his say, a happy word that he did not think he was destined to utter. Ideas have circulated; people have learned a story that they did not know, an interesting detail; they are still laughing about someone's mad idea, the charming innocence of that young girl, the witty persistence of that old scholar, and it happens that, without premeditation, and without a plan for conversation, they have talked.

    ~ Madame de Girardin, salonkeeper known as the Tenth Muse

In many places on the globe, particularly in Africa, the West Indies, and the Pacific Islands, oratorical skills are the key to political power, humorous play with language is an avenue of advancement in society, and achieving consensus through conversation is the foundation of community harmony. Not so among Americans. We grow up using language, but few of us have learned to enjoy it for its own sake or have much appreciation and understanding for its most cultivated social form, conversation. If we have any education in verbal interaction, it's likely to be through that metaphor of war called debate. We're taught how to use words strategically to attack an opponent's weak points, to defend our opinions, and to shoot down someone else's ideas. We are expected to bring the opponent around to our way of thinking or concede defeat.

Salons give us a chance to explore other ways of conversing. Salonist Ted Harris expressed the possibilities when he sent a letter to his salon members: "[I want] to know each of you," he wrote, "to study and appreciate your character, to learn from what has happened in your life, or in things that you have heard that have mattered to you. I want your passion, not your debating ability, nor your conversation-dominating/stopping ability. I want your conversation-inspiring ability."

Suppose, as Harris suggests, we entered conversations not to persuade others, but to learn about them. Imagine how different life would be if, instead of competing in conversation, we were taught to value speaking itself. Suppose we approached conversation aesthetically, looking for elegance, beauty, and simplicity. Suppose we appreciated charismatic and creative delivery and became engaged and transported by words exchanged. Suppose we listened to discover the whole, complex beauty of others' ideas, instead of picking out flaws. We might become wiser and more eloquent. We also might come to know more about humanity and the world.

> **S**uppose we approached conversation aesthetically, looking for elegance, beauty, and simplicity. Suppose we listened to discover the beauty of others' ideas, instead of picking out flaws.

The rules of debate are clear and relatively rigid, while conversation is a fluid, ephemeral art form. Cultivating it means a lot more than taking in words and ideas. It also means feeling the elusive emotions that sweep through the group, hearing the tone of voice that sparks a seemingly illogical digression, seeing the eye and hand signals that halt a monologue or applaud an observation, or feeling the sudden excitement as a quiet person in the back of the room comes forth with a powerful insight. Even those present during the conversation may not comprehend all of its nuances.

How can you cultivate this kind of conversation?

- Take risks. Reveal a little more of yourself than you normally would. Share your observations, even when they don't fit snugly with your sense of reality or your political beliefs. Don't shy away from contradictions, ambiguities, or unpredictable reactions.
- Assume some responsibility for making the conversation work. Intervene subtly when it appears to be going awry. Stop talking when

you've been holding forth too long. If someone hasn't spoken, ask her a question. Suggest a ten-minute break, point out a digression, ask for clarification.

- Practice speaking. At the great salons, guests gave thought to the act of speaking and the words chosen. They appreciated one another's wit and intelligence, and freely applauded and critiqued each other's skills. Conversation is a skill that improves with practice. Don't be afraid to think up and save bon mots for the right moment. Keep a pen in hand during the salon and write down what you'd like to say when there's an appropriate opening. Sprinkle in quotes and proverbs. Tell an apt joke or an anecdote. If you believe you are a dull speaker, start studying language. Pay attention to the dialogue in movies, go to plays, listen to recorded books, read poetry aloud to yourself. As you become more alert to the nuances of the spoken word, your own words will gain elegance and impact.

- Listen and glean. Savor the witticisms, insights, pet phrases, or newly coined words you hear. Write them down, include them in your newsletter, try them out for yourself.

- Reflect. Go back over the actions or words that influenced the group. What kinds of interactions occurred and who furthered them? How was this meeting different from the last one, or from conversations a year ago? What did you most enjoy, and what triggered your enjoyment? What contributed to intimacy, trust, and solidarity in the salon? Where was the play, fun, and risk? What was most intellectually stimulating or politically provocative?

TOUCHSTONES OF GOOD SALON CONVERSATION

BREVITY

Brevity is the soul of lingerie.

~ Dorothy Parker

"The noise of those who speak too much is just as bothersome as the silence of those who hardly speak," cautioned Madame de Scudéry. The time constraints of modern schedules make brevity compulsory in many situations; in the salon, if everyone is to have a say, then everyone must be as concise as possible. Those who are not brief must at least be entertaining.

If the members of your salon have trouble being succinct, you might try imposing a time limit on each contribution for a few sessions. Keeping track of time forces people to condense their ideas into fewer (and more powerful) words. Three- to five-minute limits generally work best. Choose ten minutes if your salon's style just won't stand for such brevity, or if you are discussing subjects that require a great deal of background information. Asking your most loquacious member to take the job of timekeeper can enhance his or her awareness of time.

Dorothy Parker

Another way to cultivate brevity is condoning vigorous interruptions. Though interruption is not the accepted standard in the United States, it can be a natural and energetic way of cutting down on loquacity. (Interruptions are standard behavior in the West Indies, where conversation is boisterous entertainment as well as a means of communication and decision.) It's also more flexible than the somewhat mechanical time-limit method, in that skillful and to-the-point speakers are generally allowed to finish, while those who drone on without direction are soon called to account.

Granted, the interruption method may favor those with domineering personalities, but it also may compel quieter members to become more skilled and assertive—the way a child learns to compete successfully for attention in a large, talkative family.

Is there such a thing as too much brevity? Perhaps not. The nth degree of brevity is silence, which, in its deliberation and peacefulness, can be a positive contribution to conversation.

CLARITY AND SPECIFICITY

Don't, Sir, accustom yourself to use big words for little matters.

~ Samuel Johnson

At its best, salon speech is not only brief and to the point, but also straightforward and clear, avoiding specialized jargon, convoluted grammar, and obscure references. It's exact speech that says what it means. In the words of Mark Twain, "The difference between the right word and the nearly right word is the difference between lightning and the lightning bug."

Concreteness and specificity are just as important. Vague, broad statements lead to thoughtless agreement or antagonism. Salonist Ted Harris has found that, when salon members fail to ground their statements in specifics, particularly personal observation, the discussion inevitably morphs into wobbly general arguments, in which, as he puts it, "every statement is loaded with unshared assumptions and methods." Whenever possible, use examples to illustrate your meaning. Tell stories, relate events, give details, make analogies, tangle with paradoxes. Remember: You speak so that you may be understood.

ORIGINALITY

Originality consists in thinking for yourself, not in thinking unlike other people.

~ J. Fitzjames Stephen, English jurist

The more specific you are, the more original you will become. Anyone can proffer a generalization, but when you value, reflect upon, and draw conclusions from your own life experiences and allow others to challenge you, you enter the realm of original thought.

The best salons encourage the expression of original ideas by learning to recognize the assumptions and reflexive reactions that stifle freshness. More concretely, you can deliberately choose topics that encourage the expression of unusual ideas and experiences. You might hold a salon session titled "Pet Theories." Just about everyone has developed a few unorthodox notions that may or may not be supported by facts. You can turn them into in-jokes or shared history by keeping a list of them or publishing them in your newsletter, where they'll stand as a symbol of your salon's commitment to originality.

Another topic that elicits original responses is "Great Business Ideas"—concepts or inventions that would be enormously successful if only someone with the proper resources were willing to take a risk on them. "Childhood Revelations and Experiments" lets salonists share youthful insights, which are almost by definition daring and original— how you discovered that Santa Claus was a front for your parents' gift-giving; your first lies and their consequences; your first truly adult feeling. A session devoted to brainstorming on absolutely any subject can also trigger innovation. Brainstorm unusual solutions to a particular world problem, then brainstorm further about how to actually implement these solutions. You could find yourselves at the forefront of a new social movement—it's been known to happen in salons before.

TACT

Tact is a beautiful quality because it is based on kindness.

~ Margaret Anderson

Tact is subtle sensitivity to the interpersonal dynamic, combined with genuine appreciation of other people's talents and experiences. It requires a degree of detachment—the ability to see a situation as it is without needing to impose a solution on it. According to Alabama salonist D.S. Lodge Peters, the essence of tactfulness is "knowing when to shut your mouth instead of hollering about your Great-I-Am."

CECIL BEATON USED WITH PERMISSION OF SOTHEBY'S

Emerald Cunard, by Cecil Beaton

In practice, it's about finding ways to resolve difficulties between people without putting anyone on the spot. Someone in your salon clearly wants to speak—he's shifting in his chair, eager and anxious, but hasn't found a way in yet. Instead of shining the spotlight of attention on him, you could simply say, "I'd really like to hear from people who haven't spoken yet." You haven't forced him to say anything (he can still remain silent), nor have you criticized anyone for monopolizing the conversation. Now it's the responsibility of the person who wanted to speak to seize the opening.

The average contemporary salonist is, luckily, unlikely to be called upon to exercise the degree of tact that Emerald Cunard displayed when she introduced the Prince of Wales to one of her more colorful friends. To everyone's horror, the friend took out a small gun and placed it on the table in front of him. Regicide or suicide? Lady Emerald picked up the pistol with a studiedly casual air. "Oh, what an elegant object. Is it loaded with black pearls?" she asked, and dropped it into her purse.

Tactful intervention is based on patience. Wait, take a few breaths, and evaluate your own motives before you make a move. If you suggest a change, do so as unobtrusively as possible, preferably without causing a break in the conversation. Frame your concerns as your own, without attempting to speak for everyone else. If you hear a sigh of consensus or a murmur of agreement pass through the group, you may decide to press your point a little more firmly. Be aware that even tactful suggestions can incite conflict.

Tact shouldn't be used as an excuse to sidestep confrontations that could actually lead to deeper mutual understanding, nor as a form of hyperpolite one-upmanship. And if you tend to be quiet and passive anyway, cultivate outspokenness and passion—tact will take care of itself.

SINCERITY

Great thoughts come from the heart.

~ Marquis de Vauvenargues

Sincerity can make up for a lack of all other conversational skills. An earnest willingness to express one's emotions honestly invites others to discard their masks and conventions, so that real concerns and raw feelings can be revealed. It's a radical act.

And despite its emotional warmth, it can set people at ease even as it energizes them. Salonist Marco Ermacora says that one powerfully honest conversation "created some critical mass, and all this energy was released. I hadn't felt so relaxed in a long time."

In short, the salon comes most alive when each person's essence and charisma shine forth. Those who are afraid to be seen as fools or idealists stifle themselves and others in the group. Sincerity means taking risks and not policing yourself for consistency. "Mme de Staël is sincere in innumerable contrary ways in succession," wrote her admirer Benjamin Constant, "but as in each moment of speaking she is really sincere, one is overcome by the accent of truth that echoes in her words."

Ask your questions, then. You may elicit answers that someone else desperately needs. Reveal the truth of your life, because you may reveal to others their own truths. Discuss your doubts, because in doing so you may allow others to share theirs. Tackle taboo subjects. Allow your passions to guide you. Let your voice ring with energy and excitement.

> **T**he salon comes most alive when each person's essence and charisma shine forth. Sincerity means taking risks and not policing yourself for consistency.

If there is a downside to sincerity, it is exemplified by people who bring up the same subjects repeatedly, no matter what everyone else is talking about. Tact is unlikely to inhibit such a fanatic, and tolerance exacts a heavy toll. Tackle the problem head-on, perhaps asking the person not to mention the overworked subject for at least three meetings and recalling that all salon members have agreed to explore many perspectives and many issues. Most fanatics will recognize that they've overdone it, and back off. The others will probably abandon the salon for a more submissive venue.

LIGHTHEARTEDNESS, WIT, AND HUMOR

But beyond all that I have said, I also want a certain joyful spirit to reign there, that . . . inspires in the heart of each member of the group a disposition to enjoy everything and not to be bored by anything; and I want great and small things said, provided they are always well said.

~ Madeleine de Scudéry

Sincerity is crucial, but unrelenting earnestness can lead to a level of intensity that simply wears people out. Throughout time, laughter has pervaded salons. A ready, witty epigram has been the traditional calling card of the salon guest. "To be wildly enthusiastic, or deadly serious—both are wrong. Both pass," said the novelist Katherine Mansfield, a frequent salon guest of Lady Ottoline Morrell. "One must keep ever present a sense of humor." Lightheartedness made salons a pleasure to attend—and it can do the same for yours, of course.

A playful spirit doesn't necessarily imply a lack of seriousness. The enthusiasm, energy, and open-mindedness that lightheartedness fosters are indispensable tools for the most serious problem-solving—in the wide world and within the salon itself. When salon conversations come to an uncomfortable halt, it may mean that your group is focused too intensely on one perspective or one approach to your topic. A lighthearted remark can remind members that other perspectives exist—and away the conversation goes, in a whole new direction.

"No, you're not too late. Cathy's just beginning
to put calcium into perspective."

The truth is, humor is a sign of creative, flexible minds at play, as Germaine de Staël knew very well: "Wit lies in recognizing the resemblance among things which differ and the difference between things which are alike," said the great salonist, who herself had one of the finest minds of the nineteenth century. Wit springs forth when unusual connections are made between words and concepts. Humor turns reality around, making normality seem malleable and fundamental beliefs a bit less fundamental. Humor facilitates a change of perspective. Pinpointing the contradictions and absurdities inherent in virtually any subject helps people determine what they really think.

In some tribal cultures, humor is so important that it is considered sacred. Clowns or "contraries" ceremonially poke fun at accepted, habitual ways of doing things. They help prevent stagnation in the community and temper the excesses of people in authority. Humor can have a similar effect on salons, supporting egalitarianism and preventing self-appointed leaders from taking themselves too seriously.

Laughter is also a social glue that cements community. It reduces boredom and tension within a group while breaking down boundaries between people and forging and reinforcing strong bonds of familiarity. When everyone is laughing, everyone is—momentarily—in agreement. Assuming a tone of humorous informality with newcomers quickly brings them into the group, and well-intended teasing reminds them of the social rules.

Of all the forms of humor, the one most closely associated with salons is verbal wit. Salonists traditionally enjoy every kind of word game, including puns, rhymes, anagrams, charades, and—especially—epigrams: short, witty remarks or verses improvised on the spot. Composing perfectly apt, clever epigrams on the spur of the moment was a formidably important social skill in famous salons of the past. The best ones were spread by word of mouth or in letters, and could make their inventors famous or infamous.

Some epigrams are potent carriers of new ideas—think of Voltaire's immortal "I may not agree with what you say, but I will defend to the death your right to say it"—while others may simply be ingenious ways out of sticky social situations. The sixteenth-century French lawyer Etienne Pasquier, a salon guest of the Mesdames des Roches, found himself unequal to the group's repartee. As he was about to lose an argument, he noticed a flea perched on Catherine des Roches' breast and suggested that he would love to be in the flea's position. The mother and daughter des Roches were delighted with the conceit, and Pasquier was transformed from salon goat to salon hero in an instant. Writing poetry about amorous fleas became all the rage among salon habitués, and the poems were collected into small hand-bound books for further delectation. The flea incident became famous in salon history, while the original argument that Pasquier had been losing was, of course, forgotten.

The famous salon at the Hotel de Rambouillet in the seventeenth century was nearly obsessed with clever verbal coinages. Madame de Rambouillet and company declared themselves dissatisfied with the straightforwardness of certain French nouns—so in the language of their salon, *la main* ("hand") became *la belle mouvante* ("beautiful mover") and the easy chair was rechristened, in true salon fashion, *une commodité de la conversation* ("an aid to conversation").

Verbal play reached its height—or nadir, depending on your point of view—among the members of the Algonquin Round Table, most of whom were writers, editors, or actors with a shared love of language. Pamela Case Harriman, daughter of Algonquin Hotel manager Frank Case, relates that their favorite game was an elaborate form of punning called I-Can-Give-You-a-Sentence. "I can give you a sentence with the word *burlesque*," Alexander Woolcott might propose. Pregnant pause. "I had two soft-burlesque for breakfast."

Not all salon humor has been friendly. Eighteenth-century wit, in particular, excelled at rapier thrusts directed at one's opponent's reputation. A classic verbal battle took place at London's Beef Steak Club between John Wilkes, a journalist and politician, and rival politician Lord Sandwich. Lord Sandwich is said to have initiated the exchange by predicting that Wilkes would die "either of the pox or on the gallows."

"That," Wilkes retorted, "will depend on whether I embrace your lordship's mistress or your lordship's principles."

It takes only one ready wit in your salon to bring out the latent humor in everyone else. Laughter begets laughter and puns beget puns (like a plague, some would say). If there's no stellar comic in your salon, instigate humor yourself. First of all, laugh. Trust your personal sense of the absurd. As you express what tickles your fancy, others will come to understand you, and will feel comfortable revealing their own private amusements. When a witticism springs to mind, or when you want to try out someone else's witty remark for yourself, speak it boldly—and then let it go. Nothing is more agonizing than a repeated joke, with the pathetic implied plea for a response. Madame du Deffand, for one, would have none of it. "How much trouble he takes, how he exerts himself to be witty," she sniffed, referring to Jean-François Marmontel, a fashionable novelist and dramatist who frequented her somewhat forbidding salon. "He is only a vagabond clothed in rags!"

Not that you need to wait for humor to happen. Impersonations, parody, and prepared jokes can become salon activities—they're every bit as good as impromptu humor. You can devote entire salon evenings to reading aloud funny passages from books, sharing favorite cartoons, or telling funny anecdotes. You might also try games that encourage offbeat associations. Pull out a book on dogs, then decide which breed each of the salon members resembles. Salonist Margaret Anderson and her friends asked each member to walk across the room two or three times. "Then we would all try to evaluate that person's essence," she recalled. "Was it a dry, thin essence? Was it like a fruit with much juice?"

Even the darker kind of salon humor can become a group enterprise. A game of ironic comments and smart retorts can be great fun. On a riskier level, so can an aggressive game of trading insults; an aggressor may become a victim at the turn of a phrase. Be warned, however: Contemporary Americans can be a thin-skinned lot compared to epigram-hardened classic-salon habitués. (Even in the past, though, a sharp remark sometimes led to ill feelings and caused people to leave a salon, never to return.) If your insulting sallies are met with stony silence and averted eyes, back off. Being too protective of salon members' feelings can be smothering, but don't hesitate to call things to a halt if the laughter becomes mean-spirited. Wit that wounds and cultivates unequal relationships generally contains elements of abuse.

Wit that is racist, sexist, classist, or otherwise derides any group of people is, of course, essentially witless as well as hurtful. Minority group members may choose to make fun of themselves, but self-deprecation is risky; those who make fun of themselves may be believed. Humor is best used to lampoon those in power, to tease out paradoxes in an argument, and to gently puncture pride and posturing. As the author Aldous Huxley once said, "People are much too solemn about things! I'm all for sticking pins into episcopal behinds."

ARGUMENT

Gatherings at which feelings are never hurt are not salons, they're tea parties.

~ John Berendt, "The Salon"

One salonist presents a hypothesis. Others in the group poke at it, bring up exceptions, identify faulty premises, and otherwise test the idea, making it stronger or perhaps knocking it down altogether. It's called argument, and if it's not generally a comfortable experience, it can give life to a salon like nothing else. Argument is a great forcing-house of originality; banish it, and watch a salon grow dull.

The Marquise de Lambert kept a serious salon running during the notably frivolous and libidinous French Regency era (1715–23). Here arguments about, among other things, the authorship of the poems attributed to Homer would blaze so fiercely that they could only be brought to an end by everyone's adjourning for a champagne supper at the Restaurant Valincour.

One of the commonest complaints expressed by members of long-running salons is that the participants have all come to think alike and agree with each other, so they have nothing left to talk about. In many cases, fear that discussions may erupt into arguments inhibits them. When people are afraid that the group can't handle differences of opinion, none will be offered.

The concern can be a reasonable one. Few people are skilled debaters. Some consider argument a matter of being loud enough long enough to wear everyone else down. Others refuse to listen to other people's ideas, lest they lose a point in their favor. And still others resort to name-calling and derision.

For such people, learning to relax and enjoy a good debate calls for practice and a shift in attitude about argument. Argument doesn't have to be a struggle for self-defense or dominance. It can be an energetic way of opening yourself, and others, to possibilities you've never entertained before. Think of it as another verbal game—one that improves your mental agility and informs your opinions.

In his autobiography, turn-of-the-century journalist Lincoln Steffens describes a clever debate game he and the American impressionist painter John Henry Twachtman often played at salons and social gatherings:

> Twachtman would whisper to me as he passed on to his place, 'I'll say there can be no art except under a monarchy.' Waiting for a lull in the conversation, he would declare aloud his assertion, which was my cue to declare the opposite. 'You are wrong, Twachtman. Art is a flower of liberty and blossoms only in republics.' Others would break in on his side or mine and, marking our followers, he and I led the debate, heating it up, arousing anger—any passion, till, having everybody pledged and bitter on a side, we would gradually change around till he was arguing for the republic, I for the monarchy. Our goal was to carry, each of us, all our party around the circle without losing a partisan. The next night Twachtman would whisper and later declare that 'Foreign women are not beautiful; only American women have real beauty,' and again we would try to lead our heelers around to the opposite view. It was amazing how often we could do it.

In general, an argument is best conducted within the conversational guidelines we've already discussed. It's far better to express disagreement through wit than rudeness; far more effective to argue with sincerity and tact than with rancor and disdain; far cleverer to debate with precision than with rambling generalizations. "I'm willing to explain, but not justify," says salonist Carol Anne Ogdin. "I'm willing to answer a question, but not a challenge; I treat every request as honest, even if it is tinged with sarcasm. I'm finding the responses I'm eliciting are rising in general quality."

When you're arguing, confine yourself to a specific, debatable topic. Nothing will come of an argument that boils down to insistence on one absolutist viewpoint. When an argument is reduced to two opposing generalizations, says salonist Ted Harris, "you often get two paralyzing situations: One is that the conversation becomes ever more abstract until we reach pure metaphysics, at which point all of the shared meanings of terms are lost. The other is a retreat to divisive pontification: for example, someone saying, 'Men and women are intrinsically different, and you must accept this!'" If your salon stumbles down this path, Harris suggests looking for "common ground from which to begin." Once your group has found a place of agreement, however narrow, you can return to the original topic, focusing on specifics rather than generalizations.

Although specificity spurs healthy debate, the "prove it" game is usually counterproductive. Don't demand a citation or source from a speaker unless you're genuinely interested in the article or reference and intend to track it down. Nor should you deride someone who supports an idea because he or she read something, but can't tell you who wrote it, when it appeared, or the title of the relevant book or magazine. It's imperative to deal with the substance of what someone is expressing; whether the person has a good memory for names, titles, or peripheral facts is virtually irrelevant.

When others argue with you, they're paying you a compliment. People rarely bother to contradict someone whose views seem stupid or inconsequential to them. Be playful, humorous, and respectful. Unless you have made a deliberate decision to allow insults, avoid vitriol. As Carol Anne Ogdin puts it, "What you gain with sarcasm and insinuation is to win the battle and lose the war."

Arguments can proceed without a plan and end without a declared winner. Over time, the subject can be examined again and again in your salon, each time from a new perspective. To avoid taking arguments too seriously, emulate Twachtman and Steffens: Play devil's advocate from time to time, or try arguing from a point of view opposed to what you really believe. The entire salon can do this on occasion. If an argument has grown too polarized, suggest that everyone reverse polarities and argue the opposite view just as vehemently. This exercise inevitably results in broader thinking about the subject and warmer mutual understanding within the group. Members quickly realize that their original position is not the only defensible perspective.

What should you do if things simply get out of hand and the argument becomes a shouting match? Try to break the tension. Do something sudden and distracting. "If you pour a glass of water over the table," writes tertulia host Ramón Gómez de la Serna with tongue in cheek, "you abate the anger of the conversation."

ACTIVE LISTENING

Listening is the foundation of a good salon. Through listening to others carefully, we are able to step imaginatively and empathetically into their shoes, and to experience the world from an entirely different point of view, if only for a few moments. Californian Shelley Kessler, who has taught council methods to elementary school students, advocates listening "between the lines" as someone speaks, "hearing the feelings and the intentions as well as the words. It requires tremendous discipline." This sort of rigorous attention to other people's speech is variously known as creative listening, active listening, or deep listening.

Active listening is not easy. For one thing, most people think about four times faster than they speak. It's easy for a listener to tune a speaker out three-quarters of the time, while rapidly turning over his or her own ideas. If you find yourself doing this, practice watching the speaker as well as listening to what is being said. Note each word and nonverbal signal, letting your mind rest during the pauses between phrases or sentences. If you regularly jump to conclusions about where someone is headed and then stop listening, discipline yourself to pay attention long enough to find out whether your assumption was correct.

Active listening also requires setting judgments and reactions aside. While listening, try to grasp the essence of what you are hearing. Ask yourself how the speaker feels about the subject, and whether her words are congruent with her body language and expressions. Look for underlying meaning rather than superficial information.

Notice which words trigger automatic reactions on your part. Emotionally charged opposites like feminine and masculine, crime and safety, or community and individualism mean quite different things to different people. When you find yourself reacting to what a speaker has said merely because a certain word was used, listen to determine whether the speaker is using the term the same way you use it. If you aren't sure, ask for clarification rather than arguing about what it means. You might also devote a salon session to a particular word or concept that often produces misunderstandings in the group. Ask each person who holds the talking stick (see chapter 9) to state the problematic word three times, then to say whatever comes to mind—an anecdote, image, or feeling. By the end of the round, repetition will have diminished the word's impact, and the images, feelings, and stories you have heard will tell the group a lot about what the word implies for different people.

There are many ways to develop the "muscle" of truly hearing another's words. Here's one: Break into groups of three. Choose a controversial topic. Ask one person to state his position on the subject for roughly five minutes, then ask number two to summarize what number one said. Then the first speaker gets to say whether she thinks the summary is accurate. Now reverse the process: Number two speaks, number one summarizes, etc. Finally, the third person, who has only been listening and observing so far, comments on what she noticed while the others were speaking and listening.

Or have your group listen to two members discuss a "hot" topic, and then, as a group, discuss what it is about language, speaking styles, and mannerisms that makes listening easy or difficult. This is a powerful way to learn about both speaking and listening.

As your salon or council members become adept listeners, you may find it hard to accept new members who haven't developed your skills of stillness and attention. California salonist Bert McNutt says that newcomers to his salon often seem "very talkative and have a lot to say, but are restless when it is their turn to listen. They tend to interrupt a lot, and most never make a second meeting." In your first contact with potential new members, explain what you are trying to do as a group and the styles of speaking and listening that you have developed. If you need to, conduct a listening exercise each time a new person attends.

When you listen deeply to others, you may find yourself without anything clever or moving to say when your turn comes around. But this lack of preparation is a blessing in disguise; it gives you access to spontaneous and heartfelt words. Whether you're engaged in council or conversation, remember to take a deep, slow breath and to allow several seconds to pass before speaking. Restate the central issue in your mind, so you aren't limited by, or simply reacting to, the previous person's comments. Now say whatever springs to mind. Let go of the great thoughts you had while others were speaking. If nothing comes to mind, take another deep breath, and another, until something wells up. As your group becomes accustomed to active listening and unprepared speaking, you'll find everyone's words growing in feeling, meaning, and impact.

CHAPTER EIGHT

KEEPING THE SALON RUNNING:

LEADERSHIP, FACILITATION,

AND RULES

In several of the successful groups the "leader" was more of a presence than a person . . . a role that was taken up only when the group seemed to need it and usually by one person in particular, but occasionally by someone else. The nominal leaders of these groups often spoke of some identifiable chemistry being the bottom line for "what works": They spoke of groups that were able to bond around a core of members who were committed and persistent in their intent to make it work, open-minded enough to let things happen, and respectful of people even if their opinions were contrary to their own. In turn, these qualities often emanated from a group because the "leader" projected them.

~ Lorraine Suzuki, Southern California salonist

A community is like a ship; everyone ought to be prepared to take the helm.

~ Henrik Ibsen, *An Enemy of the People*

The great salons may have been democracies of talent and intellect, but they were usually monarchies when it came to leadership. Mesdames du Deffand and Geoffrin (two of the more directive salon divas, to be sure) didn't merely originate their salons, they reigned over them, subtly but firmly enforcing the rule of wit and good manners. Julie de Lespinasse was more like a smiling, still center than a lawgiver—but she too was the undisputed queen of her gatherings.

This autocratic principle sometimes led to what can most charitably be called overorganization. Jean Antoine de Baïf hosted a sixteenth-century salon that was highly successful, but with which he was displeased. He felt that it, and the other salons of his day, lacked focus and direction. In an attempt to create a salon whose seriousness was beyond question, he sought—and won—the backing of King Charles IX for what would eventually come to be called the Académie du Palais, or Academy of the Palace. This gathering set as its goal the reform of French poetry and the purification of the French language, and for a while it thrived. But under the succeeding king, Henri III, the Académie became more and more formal, duller, drier, and more academic. Soon palace wits were satirizing the boring goings-on. Salongoers then, as now, preferred free conversation to stiff, academically respectable readings or lectures.

These salons flourished and foundered in an age of absolutism. In our more democratic time and nation, the autocratic salon is, perhaps luckily, a hard act to put over. Members generally want a say in the direction the salon is taking, and they may drop out if one person exerts too much control. If the individual running things is perceived as more dynamic and impressive than the other group members, the salon can turn into a sort of personality cult, in which the opinions of the leader

In *Reading Molière* (ca. 1728), by Jean François de Troy, an early-eighteenth-century salon is held by the words of the great French dramatist

become orthodoxy and the needs of the group are ignored. At the very least, the single person who has carried the salon on his or her shoulders may begin to resent all the unacknowledged work and drop out, leaving the salon leaderless and in a shambles.

For these reasons and others, it's usually best for several or all members to share leadership responsibilities. Toward this end, you can divide "official" leadership tasks so as to include as many people as possible.

The leaders within a salon fall into two broad categories: those who handle organizational details (hosts) and those who handle group dynamics (facilitators). In some salons, one person does both. In others, these roles are distinct—the host provides a place to meet, while the facilitator initiates the conversation, asks questions to keep it going, interrupts if someone talks too long or digresses too much, and so on. The host may remain constant, while the facilitator changes with each meeting, or vice-versa.

You can divide the host's responsibilities into *host* pure and simple (provider of the place), and *convenor*, who's in charge of finding new members, sending out invitations, and keeping track of the mailing or phone list. Or subdivide the convenor job into: a contact person, who keeps track of visitors and newcomers to the salon; a recruiter, who advertises for new members; a scribe, who creates and mails your salon newsletter or flyers; and a treasurer, recording donations used for postage, food, and other expenses. Other people might be in charge of cleaning up after meetings, bringing food, arranging for child care, or buying supplies for activities.

> **If the individual running things is perceived as more dynamic and impressive than the other group members, the salon can turn into a sort of personality cult.**

The facilitator's duties, too, can be subdivided. If your salon has problems with group process, you may want to create several processing roles: a timekeeper; a designated includer, who calls on people to ensure that everyone has a chance to speak; a summarizer, who restates and lists ideas as they are presented; and a checker, who clarifies statements, reminds people of agreed-upon rules of behavior, and asks questions. Some groups, when they're dealing with particularly difficult topics or problems, nominate a supporter or acceptor, who gives sincere, positive feedback and restates negative assertions in an affirmative style. One salon appoints a "vibes watcher," who defuses tension in the salon by stating the facts of group process clearly and reminding everyone to breathe deeply and acknowledge each other's feelings.

However you apportion official leadership responsibilities, everyone in the salon should have plenty of opportunity to practice the skills of effective, democratic leadership. Organizing group activities, recruiting members, maintaining communications, listening respectfully to others, seeking creative solutions, motivating group action, reconciling conflict, and gauging when to intervene and when to let things run their course—these leadership skills can be practiced, quietly or overtly, by all salon members all the time. (Particularly skillful people may serve as models for the group, of course.) Everyone should be encouraged to step in when problems arise. As facilitator Glenda Martin says at her book groups, "All have the responsibility, not just me, to say 'I don't like the way things are going' or 'Can we move on?'"

In any case, leadership should not be covert or assumed. If you opt for the single-leader model, that leader should be acknowledged openly and held accountable when the salon succeeds or fails. This allows each member to choose on an informed basis whether he or she wants to be part of the salon as it has been put together.

And it's wise to rotate the tasks among members, in order to prevent hierarchies and factions from forming and to prepare members for keeping the salon going if key people leave. New Jersey salonist Terri Schiesser points out that salons can hit the doldrums when core members grow tired of leading and new members haven't yet developed the self-confidence and sense of belonging to volunteer for leadership. If old-timers actively welcome newcomers, encourage them to assume leadership roles, and reassure them that leadership isn't prohibitively difficult or time consuming, the problem can be averted. If you let new people know what to expect and offer some guidance, they are usually eager to help out.

FACILITATION SKILLS

Leadership is something you do to a group; facilitation is something you do with a group.

~ The Center for Conflict Resolution, Madison, Wisconsin

Of all the salon leadership roles, facilitation can be one of the trickiest—and most rewarding. As facilitator, you really are stepping into the shoes of the great salon leaders of the past, who were renowned for their skill in keeping egos soothed and conversations going.

Who is the facilitator? Often, when salons choose a topic for a specific meeting, a member with an interest in the topic volunteers to facilitate. Other salons prefer to choose disinterested facilitators who are free to concentrate fully on group dynamics. Most salons change facilitators every time the salon meets. Some groups, however, find that allowing a member to facilitate two or three consecutive meetings provides practice and time for reflection.

One Connecticut salon that meets monthly rotates its facilitators this way: Each meeting is handled by a facilitator and a co-facilitator. One month's co-facilitator becomes the next month's facilitator, and the new co-facilitator is chosen on an alphabetical basis. Everyone thus plays a facilitating role for two consecutive months. If your salon meets more frequently, you may want to let each facilitator serve three times in a row—once to observe and try things out; a second time to refine his or her abilities and take greater risks; and a third time to see how the refinement has affected group dynamics.

Being a facilitator means agreeing to pay extra attention to group dynamics and trying to keep the conversation flowing. Facilitation literally means "to make easy." In the case of a salon facilitator, what ought to be made easy is communication. This requires the exercise of what we might call social or interpersonal intelligence—an aptitude for getting along with and understanding other people. True social intelligence is closely related to a gift for listening.

From an egotistical perspective, facilitating may not seem terribly rewarding. You'll have fewer opportunities to contribute your own observations because you are trying to monitor the moods of other participants. As you try to assess what's going on with each individual, you're also trying to move the group steadily toward the session's goals, what-

> **T**he first rule of facilitating is simple: Do as little as possible. The best facilitator is more of a presence than a participator: alert, focused, and injecting energy into the group, but otherwise mostly quiet.

ever they may be. Members may blame you if you intervene often, or not often enough. And yet practicing this subtle set of skills brings a world of benefit to the salon and, ultimately, a great deal of satisfaction to the facilitator.

The first rule of facilitating is simple: Do as little as possible. The best facilitator is more of a presence than a participator: alert, focused, and injecting energy into the group, but otherwise mostly quiet. Mabel Dodge admitted that she generally sat quietly at her salons, smiling in the background. Yet journalist Lincoln Steffens told her, "You attract, stimulate, and soothe people, and men like to sit with you and talk to themselves! You make them think more fluently, and they feel enhanced." That doesn't mean facilitators should simply nod, listen, and smile all the time, but the ability to do so when appropriate is a valuable, and insufficiently acknowledged, skill.

If you spot a potential problem, wait and see if anyone else notices it, or whether it will resolve itself without intervention. Good facilitators trust themselves, but they also trust the group and its unaided strengths.

Once you have intervened, say the professional facilitators at Rapid Change Technologies, Inc., an organizational development consulting firm based in Arizona and Minnesota, you should "take a hundred deep breaths before making another intervention, especially if you tend to be quick and articulate. Long before you reach the hundredth breath, members will have understood that you really mean to hear them, that you will listen. Be prepared for a flood of new energy."

Julie de Lespinasse, through charm, kindness, and adroit attention, was able to prevent the formidable philosophe (and great talker) d'Alembert from dominating the conversation in her salon. In our own day, professional mediators and facilitators have developed many ways to intervene subtly, without affecting the flow of talk. Two of the most useful are body language and compliments. Eye contact is powerful body language. A determined monologist will often fall silent if you break off eye contact with him, and you can cue others to speak by deliberately glancing in their direction. You can acknowledge and encourage a speaker by a steady, alert gaze.

You can also employ more obvious body signals. A wink, a squint, or a raised eyebrow can lighten the mood of the salon and bring the group into greater intimacy. Leaning forward or backward, sitting with crossed arms, and nodding or shaking your head—all of these gestures send messages. Try one or two physical signals during each salon meeting, and notice the effect. A word of warning, though: Interpretations of gestures and tone of voice vary widely throughout the country and the world. (Some people regard eye contact, for example, as intrusive or domineering.) Experiment by increasing your use of nonverbal tools in subtle increments, remaining alert to reactions that indicate discomfort.

Offering praise is another good means of bringing people into greater intimacy and trust—as long as it isn't faked, automatic, effusive, trivial, or too general. It should be person- and incident-specific: "That was fun, Bob," is virtually meaningless, but "You really have a knack for expressing complicated ideas simply" is a remark that skillfully acknowledges a person's real abilities.

No matter how well things are going, keep challenging yourself with questions: How can I be sure everyone is as involved as they would like to be? Has everyone expressed what they want to get from the group? How might the salon be changed so it more closely meets the needs and expectations of members? Are other people involved in cofacilitating? Why or why not? How can I do a better job of modeling respect for people's feelings, sensitivities, and beliefs?

Participate in groups where you are not the facilitator. Notice how others handle the same dynamics you deal with in your group. When you think you aren't having enough opportunities to take part, or aren't being accorded respect in these groups, ask yourself what you would do if the situation were reversed.

RULES OF BEHAVIOR

We've forgotten how to be together. Salons or salonlike gatherings are what humans have done since before recorded history. Our ancestors developed all kinds of rules and signals and etiquette that facilitated being together in groups. We've lost those social skills. We need to rediscover them, partly from other cultures and partly from our own fumbling, awkward experience.

~ Eric Utne

Achieving a consensus on standards of behavior for a salon is a fundamental exercise in social intelligence — and the process enhances every salon member's facilitation skills into the bargain. Behavioral rules are simple, practical tools to ensure civility. Alabama salonist D.S. Lodge Peters has found that tolerance may be difficult to instill, but "civility [is] another matter. 'Please,' 'thank you,' and sweet silence in the face of scoldings [can] be taught and learned formally and by example." Once established, behavioral standards help people relax their critical scrutiny of one another and eliminate some of the friction among diverse personalities. Accepted standards are part of what binds individuals into friendship and community.

Of course, agreeing on which behaviors to encourage is a delicate process. Keep in mind that all behavior is both culturally influenced and open to individual interpretation. What one person considers simple politeness may seem like inhibition to someone else. For some quiet souls, any sort of argument is offensive, while others consider forceful argument their favorite form of intellectual stimulation. Some have never learned how to listen to others without framing a contrary opinion; others listen too well, hesitating to voice their own thoughts. This variety shouldn't come as a surprise. After all, "acceptable behavior" comes in many forms, from the shouting, laughing insults of West Indian women at market to the restrained delicacies of formal Japanese speech.

Given such varied and even contrary notions of "good behavior," you'll want to be careful about the rules you establish and the ways you put them into practice. Insist on civility, but don't use your standards as an excuse to stifle different ways of talking and behaving. Instead, seek to expand your range of behavior as a group. Establish rules that give all your salonists the opportunity to practice their values in respectful relationships with one another.

How? Well, the first principle of effective and flexible rule making is to have as few rules as possible. Work to make your behavioral standards simple and easy to put into practice. People generally regulate themselves once they know what is expected and appreciated, provided the rules are fair and allow for personal eccentricity—and if they themselves took part in drafting them. Whatever guidelines you adopt, consider doing so only experimentally, perhaps for three meetings at a time. Then evaluate how well they're working.

Here are a couple of examples of salon rules that are reasonable, humane, and easily enforced. If your salon has members who try to maintain conversational dominance by continually rerouting the discussion to their favorite subjects or their own life stories, you might agree as a group that, in order to stay on topic most of the time, you'll establish a rule that anyone can interrupt the speaker to ask how his or her point is relevant to the subject. Some salons find it necessary to establish the "no side conversations" rule. To be sure, a certain amount of side conversation is natural and inevitable, especially among people who feel at ease with each other. It can even be a source of amusement or take the conversation in an entirely new direction. But if the chat is disruptive, the facilitator can glance at the side talkers or ask one of them a question, or a neighbor can give them a friendly nudge—securely backed by everyone's knowledge of the rule.

Once your rules are established, be certain that a problem really exists before you attempt to address it with new rules. For example: Suppose one or two people dominate most of the conversations at your salon. You're concerned that others in the group are not getting the chance to express themselves. Before you propose a solution to what you consider a problem, find out whether others agree with you. Perhaps the loquacious members are gifted storytellers and original thinkers who stimulate the other members, and the quiet ones are perfectly content. If so, there's no need to create rules that might inhibit the group. Instead, when you feel that someone has been speaking for too long, gently interrupt the talker. Or suggest that the salon set time limits for comments—a procedural rather than a behavioral rule.

If, however, your group experiences frequent discussion meltdown and all agree that something has to change, hold a meeting (at a different time than your usual gathering) to discuss what might be done. Rather than complaining about one another, brainstorm a list of "problem" ways of behaving that you've noticed aren't helping the group. Often, simply voicing the problems will change behavior in the group without naming, punishing, or ostracizing anyone. If that doesn't seem sufficient, tackle each problem separately, again without shame or blame. Then lay out explicit rules. Keep in mind that rules are made to be internalized, then forgotten—salon conversation should eventually become a free-flowing, ecstatic, and unself-conscious act.

TOLERANCE AND CONFLICT

[These are] evenings dedicated to the art of conversation, where we can meet our neighbors and hear what moves the people we rub shoulders with on the bus, where—for a couple of hours, at least—all judgment is suspended, and we are free to speak without fear of being rated or told we are wrong, without needing to convince . . .

> ~ Salonist Camille Stupar, describing the café salons in San Francisco

It wasn't for me to reconcile different points of view.

> ~ Mabel Dodge

San Francisco salonist Ruthe Stein says:

My fellow book club members happen to think highly of their opinions. More often than I would have thought, those opinions are not the same as mine. So we have a situation in which a group of people who have always gotten along suddenly find themselves having words once a month. . . . We have had to learn [that] it is okay to have divergent points of view—that, in fact, the best discussions are the ones in which we differ the most.

Stein's remarks underscore the inevitability—and the advantages—of conflict in salons. This inevitability is one of the reasons that it's unwise to clutter up a salon with too many rules. You're seeking community, and healthy community includes diversity. The salon is a place for new perspectives, not an enclave of the like-minded. Salons give us the opportunity to become less sensitive to slights, more open to tactful criticism of our behavior, and better able to accept casual scrutiny of our opinions. They are, or should be, laboratories of tolerance.

A tolerant group allows everyone to say what they really think and feel, comfortable in the assurance that they will be respected even in the face of disagreement. This comfort is partly a group responsibility. All members must work to ensure that no one is cast aside. A warm, friendly group that welcomes and accepts each member can get away with teasing, jokes, and honest feedback that might devastate an individual if he or she were in a different environment. Tolerance includes enjoying the give-and-take of conversation, and trusting that others will not be personally offended by your statements but will cheerfully argue if you get too outrageous.

You can practice tolerance on an individual level by thinking before you speak. If you flare up internally in response to someone's remarks, set aside your first, probably defensive reaction and wait for a deeper response to emerge. Put yourself in the speaker's place, and allow your imagination free rein. Ask yourself if the remarks are touching a subject you are reluctant to face. If an idea upsets you, consider the consequences of adopting it for a time. Enjoy the novelty value of this "impossible" notion. If you are being teased, consider it a form of acknowledgment. If you have been the victim of a particularly sharp tongue, consider the possibility that the wound was not intentionally inflicted.

You needn't become so easygoing that you abandon your opinions. Trust your own ideas and feelings, and demand respect for them if necessary. If a fellow salonist taunts you repeatedly, take her aside. Let her know that her comments bothered you, and ask her to pay more attention to the implications of her words. Most offenders are surprised and apologetic when they're approached this way. For the truly combative, who enjoy making others squirm, firmer measures are called for: perhaps a raised eyebrow and a haughty tilt of the head, or a witty retort in the classic salon style.

What happens if you really can't stand someone—if an apparently unresolvable personality conflict makes attending the salon an agonizing experience, and you've tried your best to sit in that person's skin? The issue should be aired in the salon. Given wise, neutral facilitation, sufficient honesty, and essential respect for others, the group can probably get at the root of the problem and negotiate some kind of reconciliation—though the two of you may never become friends.

Personality conflicts are not the only ones that salons have to deal with, of course. Conflict can arise from any number of sources: arguing about the topic, arguing about the process, or arguing about how to run the group. It may emerge from differing needs and goals, attempts by some members to "prove" themselves or attract others, or power struggles. Sometimes the facilitator's main job is trying to figure out what the conflict is really about, for the expressed problem may be quite different from the underlying tensions.

Some people may feel that any conflict whatsoever indicates that the facilitator isn't doing a good job. But a willingness to deal with differences and even yell a bit may be the only way to move beyond "ideas about ideas"—and into the feelings and values behind them. When people truly reveal themselves, even (or especially) while disagreeing, they discover commonalities that bring them together in a powerful way. If they are afraid to say what they really think, the result is boredom—a far more common cause of group breakup than conflict.

Of course, some groups have no desire to become intimate. Straightforward intellectual conversation is all the participants want, and they prefer to maintain a polite demeanor under all circumstances. Such a group provides a pleasant social outlet without the risk inherent in emotionally charged discussions. Other groups may view conflict as part of the participants' commitment to reaching deeper levels of mutual understanding.

When a conflict arises, the facilitator should first describe his observations and feelings as clearly and nonjudgmentally as possible. Avoid singling people out; instead, point out changes in group behavior and mood. It's generally not a good idea to apply the techniques practiced in therapeutic, self-help, or spiritual groups. You are not there to provide therapy, only to encourage others to work together, listen to one another, and find their own solutions. Ask the others to describe their feelings and responses to what's going on. The more honest you are initially, the more likely it is that others will openly voice their concerns. In most cases, this allows you to get at the root of the conflict. Asking for other perspectives also serves as a reality check—sometimes what you interpret as a potentially dangerous confrontation just feels like an enjoyably intense argument to everyone else.

As a group, you may want to establish specific rules for dealing with healthy conflict and preventing needless damage to the group. For example, you might decide to prohibit insults and personal attacks, thereby minimizing conflict born of name-calling. The facilitator might also be empowered to call a time-out during heated discussions. You can agree to return to the touchy subject after a break or at another meeting. Or you might allow the facilitator to change the discussion method if the group gets stuck in petty disagreement, switching to the use of a talking stick—described in chapter 9—and concentrating on narrowly defined topics that all members feel strongly about and allowing everyone to speak without interruption or cross-talk.

If you are facilitating, asking pertinent questions is also a useful way to get people thinking about the dynamics of the conflict rather than their positions in the argument. Your questions and statements should be accurate and well timed, deepening the focus of the conversation. The best questions are open-ended, and are aimed at the group rather than any individual. Examples of questions commonly posed by facilitators include:

- Have you had any personal experiences that influenced your feelings?
- Does anyone want to play devil's advocate and argue a different view?
- I don't quite understand what you mean. Can you give an example or rephrase that?
- I'd like to hear from someone who hasn't talked yet. What do you think?

Sometimes it's enough to repeat what someone has said, letting the speaker know you've truly heard the comment. Deliberately simplifying and rephrasing what someone has said may bring out a more specific, detailed response. At other times, it's helpful to summarize what everyone has been saying, then ask for confirmation or clarification.

If you come up with a question that evokes a stronger or deeper response, rephrase it slightly and try it again. This gives participants time to think and rethink the same idea, each time going deeper. On the other hand, don't badger people with questions. If a thoughtful pause occurs, don't rush to fill the silence. Each shift into greater understanding and mutual trust requires a transition, a short time-out, as people take a breath before plunging deeper.

Finally, as facilitator you aren't called upon to stifle your own natural reactions. When something is funny, laugh. If something brings tears to your eyes, let them glisten. Each time you expose your feelings, you are giving others permission to be whole and present. The risks you take as facilitator stimulate the courage and honesty that other members need to face each other. When each person in the group is seen as a whole, complex human being, the group will abandon simplistic, fixed opinions. And that approach is the key to conflict resolution.

DROPPING MEMBERS

Mrs. Montagu has dropt me. Now, Sir, there are people whom one should like very well to drop, but would not wish to be dropt by.

~ Samuel Johnson

Sometimes, the salon's best efforts at tolerance and conflict resolution fail and a more drastic action is necessary to deal with a major breakdown in communications, violent antipathy between two people, or a member who simply cannot function in the community setting. Groups that are open to the public or frequently include new members are especially likely to cross paths with someone they can't handle, who may even represent a threat to the existence of the salon: a virulent racist, a congenital harasser of women, or someone who simply won't abide by the salon's rules of civil behavior and shared discourse. (While people with "problems"—even some who might be considered mentally ill—ought not to be automatically excluded from salons, dealing with them may involve more clinical skill and patience than your group possesses.)

In these cases, you may need to bar someone from membership. It's a decision that should never be made lightly. Far from being a "victory" over a problem, exclusion, like every other kind of departure other than those due to circumstances outside of the salon, is a symptom of underlying problems that must be dealt with. Kristin Anundsen, coauthor of

Creating Community Anywhere, reflected on the implications of the situation when six members of her salon asked another member to stop coming:

> This issue, then, is not that '[So and so] is disruptive,' but that the group does not know how to deal with a disruptive member. . . . Even assuming that the member is intrinsically offensive, this is like surgically removing a cancerous tumor. If the patient never deals with the conditions that gave rise to the tumor, chances are that other tumors will appear in its place, or the disease will express itself through different symptoms. . . . If one member can give rise to so much anger—and I heard fear, too— it would seem to me that this is a signal of an imbalance or disease in the system."

As a group, give yourself one last chance to examine your motivations. Is the person in question really likely to tear the group apart? Does the salon need to work on expanding its tolerance limits instead? Are people aligning along friendship or belief lines to exclude someone?

If the exclusion is deemed to be necessary, everyone in the group should be involved in asking the person to leave, and everyone should take responsibility for the aftermath.

Author M. Scott Peck, who has written extensively on building healthy community, suggests exclusion on an interim basis. In this scenario, a group asks the disruptive member to leave for a specific period of time, after which he or she becomes eligible to return. Alternatively, the group can allow the person to return whenever he or she feels able to cooperate and participate equally in the salon. The remaining members should plan on dealing with the issues that arise after the departure, whether it's temporary or permanent. Exclusion means that the salon process has in some way ceased to be effective. Others may now feel that their own position within the group is jeopardized, especially if they act or express themselves differently from others.

In essence, shunning someone violates the spirit of community. Trust must be rebuilt, sometimes from the ground up. But if you are willing to deal with it rather than pretending that nothing significant has happened, exclusion actually becomes an opportunity for enhancing intimacy among the remaining members. Whether people leave voluntarily or are asked to leave, it may be wise to hire an outside facilitator for at least one meeting, so that all members can freely express their concerns.

PART FOUR

VARIATIONS ON A THEME:
OTHER SALON DIRECTIONS

CHAPTER NINE

STUDY CIRCLES, COUNCILS, CREATIVITY

The core of salon creativity is free conversation, but there's no reason to make that a boundary. In the course of their life, many salons will move beyond general conversation, temporarily or permanently, transforming themselves into other forms — or experimenting with the forms to add variety and energy.

STUDY CIRCLES: FROM ISSUES TO ACTIVISM

Salonists are sometimes so stimulated by their conversations — or so frustrated by a problem they're discussing — that they decide to undertake an in-depth study of the subject. Group members begin to gather, read, and discuss relevant books and articles. If the effort is focused on a particular social issue with an eye toward improving life in the larger community, the group becomes what is known as a study circle.

Because most study circles are organized around a particular issue, participants may discuss the subject more deeply than they would in short-lived, informal salon conversations. The circle typically progresses from shared personal experiences relevant to the issue to informational sessions encouraging a broader perspective, culminating in a final session in which participants determine what action they would like to undertake.

In a sense, the honorable ancestor of the study circle is the New England town meeting, established in the seventeenth century. These issue-oriented community gatherings for the purpose of discussion were later described by Thomas Jefferson as "the wisest invention ever devised by the wit of man for the perfect exercise of government."

The development of modern study circles begins, however, with the early-nineteenth-century lyceums, voluntary adult-education associations that managed to remain independent of both the educational establishment and private profit. There were 3,500 lyceums in existence by 1835, involving entire families in discussions of public issues. This pioneering experiment soon faltered, however, and ultimately became a circuit on which paid lecturers toured the country, bringing uplifting (and rarely controversial) messages to small towns, particularly in the Midwest.

Meanwhile, a religious and educational institution in western New York State gained popularity for its summer programs in the little town of Chautauqua. Families came to camp out and attend weeks of classes, lectures, and preaching. The Chautauqua Literary and Scientific Circles, begun in the 1870s, soon spread. They provided a model to young black leaders in decades following the Civil War in their efforts to edu-

The Chautauqua Literary and Scientific Circle of 1884, Chautauqua, New York

cate freed slaves quickly and effectively. By 1915 there were 700,000 correspondence enrollees and 15,000 study circles across the country. (Des Moines, Iowa, alone had thirty.) In 1904, a showman named Keith Vawter got the bright idea of combining lyceum lecturers with stage shows and classes similar to those held at Chautauqua, and putting them on the road. Before long the brown tents of the traveling Chautauqua had become the most welcome of summertime sights in thousands of communities. The road shows reached their peak in 1924, when over 30 million Americans attended in 12,000 rural communities nationwide. While urbanites in New York and Chicago talked in literary salons, much of the country was involved in this larger network of public discussion.

The traveling Chautauqua came to an end in the age of radio and the automobile, but today the Chautauqua Institution holds an ambitious summer program of lectures and discussions on contemporary topics, addresses by religious leaders, concerts, opera performances, and theater.

Study circles persisted elsewhere as well. Swedish representatives of the temperance movement, inspired by the Chautauqua while visiting the United States, returned home and started their own program in 1902. Swedish study circles were quickly subsidized and promoted by large organizations, starting with the temperance movement, the Lutheran church, and unions, and later including local and national governments, corporations, libraries, and cooperatives. Now, roughly 325,000 Swedish study circles are held each year. The well-organized, highly visible study circles today are considered an integral part of Sweden's democracy.

Americans eventually rediscovered a form of group discussion that was invented here in the first place. In an updated form, study circles now enjoy renewed popularity among citizens who seek ways to learn about politics and become involved in issues that affect their communities. Two organizations help organize community-wide study circles throughout the United States: the Study Circles Resource Center in Pomfret, Connecticut, funded by the Topsfield Foundation; and National Issues Forums (NIF), a network of study circle organizations around the country.

TACKLING ISSUES

Some salons incorporate aspects of the study circle format into their regular discussions. Others might set up a study circle for a specific period of time, advertise it to attract new members interested in the chosen topic, then invite those newcomers to attend the ongoing salon. Contemporary study circles, however, are more often formed on a community-wide basis. They've evolved into a forum for small-group deliberation on critical public issues, and their influence on society is growing. In fact, study circles are changing the communities in which we live.

The first contemporary community-wide effort began in 1992 in Lima, Ohio, as a way of easing racial tensions in this city of 50,000 and surrounding communities. As a first step, Mayor David Berger convened a multiracial task force of clergy. Study circle leaders were then trained by the mayor's office and by faculty members at Ohio State

University at Lima. Nearly a thousand community members, drawn primarily from church congregations, were recruited for the initial round of study circles, meeting in groups of ten to fifteen people to discuss race relations in the Lima area. Many of the study circles were extended beyond the prescribed time period. Researchers at the university reported significant, positive changes in attitude toward people of other races, and many rounds of study circles have followed. In the words of Mayor Berger: "Participants come out of the discussions fundamentally changed. This city will never be the same." Lima continues to pioneer citywide study circle projects, looking into violence, crime, and youth issues and drawing circle members from a wider and wider range of local organizations.

In recent years, study circle programs have been established in many other communities. Study circles from Yarmouth, Maine, to Los Angeles are now focusing on crime, violence, race relations, education, welfare reform, sustainable use of natural resources, and other important issues—and the movement is just beginning to gather steam. This forum for "dynamic democracy" holds great promise for those who feel overwhelmed by the enormity of community problems and locked out of the political system.

STARTING YOUR OWN STUDY CIRCLE

Community-wide programs involving multiple study circles often develop out of a powerful collective belief that something must be done about a specific problem. They are typically started by a community institution— a mayor's office, school board, human relations commission, church council, neighborhood association, or civic group—but any group of citizens (or any capable, determined individual) can set a program in motion. The Study Circles Resource Center offers an excellent step-by-step guide titled *Planning Community-Wide Study Circle Programs*.

Your first step involves identifying and contacting individuals who are concerned about the issue at hand. Suppose it's air and water pollution in your community. When you're recruiting your core group, try to include community leaders as well as knowledgeable professionals who have dealt with pollution. In addition to contributing information, the professionals may be able to help you obtain program sponsorship. If the core group members are not familiar with the study circle process, hold a meeting to explain how it works and how it can make a difference in your community. Alternatively, conduct a study circle with this core group, so they can experience the process firsthand.

Your group can then begin working on several fronts: recruiting participants and potential leaders, locating meeting sites in the community, finding an organization that can train facilitators, obtaining funding; and ultimately alerting the media and the community at large.

Next, hold a training session for those who have volunteered to become study circle leaders. The training could be conducted by the continuing education department of a local college, by an adult education program, or by professional mediators or group facilitators. Be certain that those who train your facilitators are familiar with the principles of non-hierarchical, democratic group processes. The Study Circles Resource Center can be a valuable source of technical assistance and advice.

When you're ready, stage a kickoff event to emphasize the importance of the issue you've taken on and to publicize the opportunity for public involvement you're providing. Publicity is the best means of attracting a diverse range of participants, and community visibility is the only way to ensure community participation.

Your core group will need to match participants, leaders, meeting sites, and schedules. You may simply be able to assign leaders to specific sites, then advertise the meeting places and times. Now you're ready to examine pollution—and perhaps to come up with meaningful solutions. Midway through the sessions, you might call a meeting for circle leaders only, in which they compare notes, discuss group interaction problems, and garner new approaches to the subject. When the sessions have been completed, hold a community meeting that includes all circle participants and leaders. This "grand finale" is a celebration of the process, a means of reporting on the process and achieving closure, and an occasion to inform participants about groups through which they can take action.

FUNDING

Unlike traditional salons, community-wide study circles often seek outside funding. Your planning group will probably need to purchase or copy study guides and supplementary reading materials. Some advertising may be necessary as well. Because circles often meet in public places, you may need to pay for use of the facilities. Training your facilitators may cost money. The costs are hardly astronomical—any small group could probably cover them with a donation of $10 or $20 per participant—but a truly representative circle needs to include the poorest members of the community, and that egalitarian ideal generally dictates a no-fees policy.

Fortunately, many organizations and companies have become interested in convening and funding study circles. A sponsoring organization may pay for meeting place rentals, study materials, and facilitator training—particularly if you will be studying an issue of interest to the organization.

In Sweden, study circle associations receive over $100 million annually in government grants. In the United States, on the other hand, federal aid is virtually nonexistent, so local businesses and community organizations are your most likely funding sources. Be aware, however, that potential funders may not be acting from purely altruistic motives. Before you accept any money, be certain that your sponsor understands the purpose of the study circles and supports the participants' freedom to choose or supplement reading materials. Determine in advance whether the sponsor requires you to present a report, summary, or other information after the circle has ended.

STUDY CIRCLE LEADERSHIP

The study circle organizer, who may or may not be the same person as the facilitator, selects reading material, recruits participants, and arranges the meeting places and times. If the organizer does not serve as facilitator, his or her job is over once the study circles begin to meet.

During the first session, the facilitator describes the study circle format, briefly reviews the reading materials, and explains any ballots or questionnaires that will be filled out at the conclusion of the process. He or she then guides discussion of the values, ground rules, and goals the group wants to adopt. Be sure to encourage all participants to talk freely about the issue at hand in a personal way. The facilitator will usually become more directive in later sessions, guiding discussion along a clear agenda in order to cover the territory within the specified time limits. Facilitators are less likely to welcome digression than in a less focused salon. They conclude the study circle by organizing the participants' opinions and recommendations into some kind of summary.

It's best for the egalitarianism and cohesion of the group if the facilitator is not an expert, professional teacher or lecturer, but it's helpful if he or she has some formal facilitation training. The focus on a single subject brings special problems. Facilitators must ensure that participants don't try to convert each other or force a premature consensus.

The facilitator may be assisted by a recorder, who takes notes on what's said and thus tracks the progress of the study circle. Writing notes publicly can slow the conversation down, but the process lets people clarify and refine their ideas as they are written. The facilitator may also ask one participant to serve as researcher or resource person to locate extra reading materials, videos, or a guest lecturer when members decide they want to learn more about a topic.

RECORDING THE PUBLIC VOICE

After a vigorous discussion, study circle participants naturally want to convey their opinions and recommendations to policy makers. This is primarily a matter of creating a written record, which can be used to let political representatives know what their constituents are thinking and how they think problems ought to be handled.

For the study circle, arriving at a summary or interpretation of the process is a form of closure. It ensures that participants are not left feeling empty or dissatisfied after several weeks of intensive discussion. It may also move the group a step closer toward community involvement and activism, especially if members are providing feedback to a sponsoring organization. Case in point: A study circle established by Oklahoma League of Women Voters members Trish Frazier and Carol Woodward created a study circle on corrections policy, including state legislators and other public officials in the conversation from the beginning, and making summaries and action point lists with the officials right in the room.

The summary can take the form of a ballot, in which participants reach a consensus endorsing one of three or four courses of action. A questionnaire used in lieu of the ballot provides more in-depth reflection on the values and issues at stake. Sometimes each participant is simply asked to reflect on the process and provide feedback about what worked or didn't work in the circle. Questionnaires were used in abbreviated study circles called Minnesota's Talking Roundtable discussions sponsored by the Minneapolis *Star Tribune*. People from the community met throughout the metropolitan area once or twice a month to discuss an issue chosen by the *Star Tribune*. The newspaper let readers know where groups were forming in their neighborhoods and whom to contact. It offered free facilitator training and provided optional reading materials and evaluation forms that participants could send to the paper. At the end of each month, the paper published information from these ballots, usually to augment a series of articles on the subject.

On the other hand, ballots run the risk of reducing complex issues to a handful of choices, and the choices may represent middle-of-the-road approaches rather than genuine alternatives. The questionnaire provided by the *Star Tribune* for roundtable discussions of racism made some unwarranted associations between race and crime. This sparked anger in one group, but also spurred some spirited and creative debate. The participants ended up rewriting the questionnaire choices. (One way to avoid focusing a discussion on just a few choices is to hand out ballots at the end of the study circle sessions, rather than using them from the beginning.)

The NIF recommends another method of eliciting opinions. At the end of a session, ask the group the five following questions:

- How has your thinking changed about the issue?
- How has your thinking changed about other people's views?
- What didn't we work through?
- What do we still need to talk about?
- How can we use what we learned in this forum?

This open-ended method encourages free and open discussion throughout the course of the study circle, but the conclusions need to be summarized clearly if you intend to present them to policy makers or the media.

> The "dynamic democracy" reflected in today's study circles gives all of us, regardless of race, religion, gender, or economic status, a chance to take part in shaping our collective future.

Of course, reading and discussion don't necessarily lead to social change or political participation. Studies in Sweden have shown, though, that long-lived study circles tend to tackle increasingly difficult, controversial issues and eventually embrace political and social activism. The "dynamic democracy" reflected in today's study circles gives all of us, regardless of race, religion, gender, or economic status, a chance to take part in shaping our collective future.

COUNCILS: HEART SPEECH AND SILENCE

We should neither be hindered from making experiments by fear or undue
caution, nor prompted by novel suggestions to ill-considered courses.
  ~ London Yearly Meeting (Quakers), *Christian Faith and Practice*

Council-style discussion has the same purpose as the study circle—to
discover a common ground, a context that can incorporate everyone's
views—but the means to this end are very different. Council is essentially
a formal, even ritualized, way of taking turns, ensuring that everyone in
the group contributes. It also includes storytelling and oratory intended
to persuade and entertain, and asks of participants that they listen deeply,
with generous hearts rather than critical minds.

The method is simple: One person speaks for a while, followed by
a period of silence. The next person's remarks may pertain to the same
topic, but they are not necessarily related to what the previous speaker
has said. There is little or no debate.

Conversational groups are experimenting more and more often with
council methods when they are making decisions, resolving interpersonal conflicts, or trying to add a spiritual dimension to meetings. Council can be a transformative experience, particularly in groups that habit-
ually fall into argument.

A contemporary *ho'oponopono*, held in a cooperative store in Honolulu

This ceremonious and spiritual way of conversing is not common in the United States, although the Religious Society of Friends, or Quakers, use it in both spiritual and business meetings, and it has a rich tradition in Native American life. (Impressed by the sacred dignity of Iroquois councils, Benjamin Franklin wrote, "To interrupt another . . . is reckon'd highly indecent. How different this is to the conduct of a polite British House of Commons, where scarcely a day passes without some Confusion, that makes the Speaker Hoarse in calling to *Order*.")

Traditional council is also practiced by native Hawaiians. The *ho'oponopono* is held after any event that represents a threat to the cohesion of an extended family: a major quarrel, for example. This traditional family council has been adapted to many modern situations and groups in Hawaii, from businesses to family courts. As healer and *ho'oponopono* scholar Mary Kawena Pukui explains it, the process works through self-scrutiny and a commitment to absolute truthfulness and sincerity. Participants thrash out "every grudge, peeve, or resentment." A leader questions each person involved without allowing any interruptions. Responses are usually directed only at the leader. When all the circumstances have been explained and all the emotions expressed fearlessly,

A funeral *hui* for a Maori soldier, held on the North Island of New Zealand

members ask one another for forgiveness, and the leader summarizes. Ideally the matter is never discussed again—a way to protect confidentiality and keep the problem from cropping up another time.

Oratory and storytelling are central to the political discussions that have taken place in African village councils for centuries. The central ritual of the Maori, a Polynesian people native to New Zealand, is the *hui*, a kind of supersalon with feasting, oratory, and many other kinds of ritual, lasting several days. Hui are called for weddings, birthdays, funerals, to honor special visitors, and at the groundbreaking for new buildings.

Instead of attempting to co-opt or appropriate the traditions of other cultures, encourage the members of your group to study their own religious and ethnic heritage for examples of storytelling, oratory, ritual, silence, taking turns, and cooperation. If your group approaches them with flexibility and imbues them with a sense of humor, you can create your own context for the use of council.

TAKING TURNS

Traditional councils are strictly structured: Members speak in a predetermined order, and for a specified period of time. Any group that gives everyone a chance to speak without interruption is adopting a simplified version of the council process. Twelve-step groups such as Alcoholics Anonymous are among the many support and recovery groups whose "no cross-talk" mode is a form of council.

Many salons use the council method as a training device, abandoning it once they have established the habit of close listening and a commitment to giving everyone a chance to speak. The salon facilitator may suggest that, for one meeting, all participants must speak (or decline the opportunity) before anyone can speak a second time.

Another approach involves dividing the room and asking people to take turns speaking from two long lines, as some Maori tribes do in the *hui*. All local speakers sit along one side of a long hall, while speakers visiting from another village sit along the other wall. The locals may speak in turn until they're finished, followed by the visiting speakers. Or the speakers may alternate from side to side, progressing down the lines.

If there's a wide age range in your group and the oldest members seem to do all the talking, you might learn from the people of Idoma, Nigeria, where council participants speak in order by age, the youngest first.

THE FISHBOWL

Another method of taking turns, particularly useful when a large group is discussing a complex, emotional issue, or when people or points of view are at odds, is called the fishbowl. Two or more people sit in the center of a circle made up of everyone else in the group. Those in the center—the fishbowl—speak in turn, and when they finish, they return to the outer ring. Anyone from the circle is now free to move to the center and speak. Participants can return to the fishbowl a second time, but most wait until everyone in the circle has had a chance to speak. The process continues until everyone is satisfied that all aspects of the issue have been aired.

This method reduces confrontation by maintaining the group's focus on one person at a time and creating a little emotional distance from a tough issue. Variations are possible: You can allow the people inside the circle to choose the speakers from the larger group, or include in the circle two "witnesses," who summarize the positions of the two contenders before others enter the fishbowl.

THE TALKING STICK

The talking stick, which is practically synonymous with the council method, is most often associated with Native American tribes. But the talking stick has been a tradition in many other parts of the world, too, including ancient Greece. Homer depicts a council of the Greek besiegers of Troy, called to try to resolve the bitter dispute between King Agamemnon and the hero Achilles over the captive woman Briseis. As the chieftains speak in turn, they pass a wand. A talking stick can be any object—a flower, a feather, a stone, a shell—signifying that the person holding it is entitled to speak without interruption. Traditionally, it's handed clockwise around the circle, as each person speaks in turn. You can pass if you have nothing to say, but it's wise to hold the

The talking stick becomes a symbol of the group's integrity and capability for spirited communication, and so can help empower the expressiveness of the individual who holds it.

stick for a few moments of silence first to see if unexpected thoughts well up from within. The talking stick can also be returned to a table by each speaker, for anyone else to pick up. The ritual object acts, almost mysteriously in some cases, to facilitate a sincere exchange of ideas and feelings.

It's that symbolic power that allows practically anything to be a talking stick. Bruce Hyde, professor of speech communication at St. Cloud State University in Minnesota, once attended a departmental retreat at which "the person who was facilitating the meeting just grabbed a Magic Marker off the blackboard and handed it to the first person. It started around. It really allowed people to express themselves fully. . . . [In an] environment where there's tension, or where people are reluctant to express themselves, it gives them freedom."

Taking turns takes time, so most salons establish a time limit—perhaps three to five minutes per speaker—when they use a talking stick. Even with a time limit, it's best to include no more than six to twelve people if you hope to go around the circle more than once.

The best way to practice council, though, is to ignore time. Try letting the circle keep going until it reaches its own conclusion, without checking the clock or fretting when someone talks at length. After all, traditional councils may last all night or continue for several days if an important community action is being considered. Among the Maori, informal family councils start after dinner and continue until dawn. These late-night discussions, which may range from personal disputes to joking banter, become increasingly uninhibited and imaginative as the night deepens.

If you would like to invite children to a salon but aren't sure how to include them in your conversations, try using a talking stick and discussing a topic relevant to their experience—what makes for a good teacher, for example. Holding the stick helps kids feel confident that they are being listened to as equals. You may be startled by the lively stories and wise observations they contribute.

RITUAL

Ritual can play a part in any sort of salon, and it can be as simple as setting aside the first fifteen minutes for introductions, recapping the last meeting, prayer, meditation, or silence. Ritual is particularly appropriate for council-style proceedings, of course, with their emphasis on the deeper aspects of conversation and communion.

In most traditional councils, a shared meal is as important a part of maintaining harmony as the discussion itself. Masks or other objects can be used as ritual representations of different attitudes and viewpoints. By putting on a mask, hat, or cloak, the council member chooses to speak for an animal spirit, a god, or some other powerful being—and, so it is believed by many Native American cultures, becomes a channel for a higher and broader wisdom.

Means of closure is even more important than the ritual opening. An abrupt conclusion can feel so anticlimactic and frustrating that council members lose their sense of cooperation and accomplishment. Many traditional councils end with short, explicit summaries of what has been discussed. Closing prayers may be offered. During these periods, council members reflect silently on what has been said and on how the new understanding they have achieved in council may benefit the wider world.

COUNCIL LEADERSHIP

The simple expedient of structured turn-taking helps guide the council, but the leader's role—setting the mood for the group and keeping it on track—is crucial as well. You may choose to use two facilitators (or "chiefs"), preferably a man and a woman. By working as a team, they reinforce the idea of partnership that underlies the council process itself. In addition to the qualities any salon leader ought to have—a sense of humor, emotional maturity, honesty, generosity, and a bit of extroversion—many councils expect leaders to have some religious training, and to view the council process as a spiritual one.

A leader may open a council meeting with prayer or silence, select the talking stick if one will be used, and remind members of the agreed-upon rules of conduct (including the all-important rule of confidentiality, which frees everyone to speak from the heart). He or she then introduces the discussion topic or the agenda for the meeting and may begin the first round by asking a question. The leader may pause for a moment of reflection, then offer the first response to the question. Leaders who start the circle in this way should model an appropriate response by being authentic and succinct. In councils that don't use a strict round, the leader may refrain entirely from responding to the questions posed, instead guiding the session by asking questions, summarizing what has been said, and calling on people.

Leaders may also rein in speakers who talk too long or whose comments are irrelevant. Quaker clerks (equivalent to council chiefs) may stand up silently to indicate when a speaker should relinquish the floor at a meeting. Someone who is regularly disruptive or aggressive may be taken aside by an experienced, elder Quaker for a private admonishment. Whatever else they may do, leaders don't lead their councils toward an outcome. Councils may not reach resolution at all. They search for inner truth, not once-and-for-all answers. Sometimes the most useful thing leaders can do is to remain silent at the end of a round, waiting until they sense that everyone is ready to continue.

Councils may designate a witness who does not take part in the discussion, but keeps an eye on group process and dynamics. At the end of the meeting, the witness describes what he has observed in general terms, without referring to individuals. The witness tells the story of the group, noting when it faltered, how it changed over time, and how close it came to achieving its aim.

FROM THE HEART

Speaking and listening from the heart means becoming aware of the source of our words, drawing upon imagination and intuition, and serving the group rather than the ego. It generally means avoiding analysis, theorizing, and debate. And it often triggers tears, anger, or exultation. The leader must be prepared to handle emotions as they emerge without allowing the group to lose its focus. Most of the time, this is a matter of listening with full attention, without probing or pushing for details. The leader may suggest that participants direct their intense feelings toward the fire or candle at the center of the circle.

Someone who is overcome by emotion should be helped to vent it for a short time, but the leader should tactfully, and privately, remind those who are constantly breaking down that frequent outbursts, even if they're genuine, tear at the delicate fabric of the council. On occasion, individuals may disclose themselves at a level that is too intimate for the group to handle. The leader can suggest that the issues involved are too large to be dealt with at that time, asking that they be deferred until the group is ready to address them.

For some, speaking authentically means speaking from the spirit. Quakers believe that the voice of God can be heard in each individual. If you have doubts about what you are about to say in council, you might ask yourself questions such as these: Will my speaking serve me? Will it serve the circle or the community? Will the bigger picture—life, the planet, the human race, all sentient beings, God—be served? This line of questioning is particularly applicable to the council chief, who models authentic speech for the entire council.

One of the special pleasures of council is its openness to metaphor, poetry, and personal or traditional stories—modes of speech that convey subtle and complex truths in subtle and complex ways. Try telling a personal anecdote in the third person—it's a good way to help others find relevance and wisdom in your words. You may even arrive at an insight you would not have discovered if you had remained directly identified with the story.

There's no need to analyze council stories. Allow them to sink into the deeper consciousness of the group and bind it together in shared understanding.

SILENCE

To be outspoken is easy when you do not wait to speak the complete truth.

~ Rabindranath Tagore

In many cultures, a silent person is regarded as more trustworthy than a facile talker. In Southern India, the Paliyan people consider verbosity abnormal and offensive. In Denmark, Sweden, and Japan, silence among friends indicates that they are at ease with each other and have no need to fill in the conversational gaps. The Quakers, who believe that God expresses himself through the entire community of believers, tend to see a member who speaks at every meeting as lacking a firm connection with God. By contrast, most Americans have grown up in a culture that regards any social silence as uncomfortable, if not downright unfriendly. Council is a way to let that attitude go.

If your salon or council is open to experimentation, you might emulate John Hudak's Silent Meeting Club in Philadelphia. Members of this discussionless salon convened at various spots around town, but refrained from talking to one another. Hudak started the group to give people a chance to simply be together without having to make the usual obligatory small talk. The result was a peaceful sense of communion. In Daisy Birch's Washington Area Artists' Salon, "we experience things physically, emotionally, visually," she says. "We share our work. There's a lot of vulnerability there when that happens. There have been times when we have lost words, when everyone in the salon realized we had moved beyond words."

Silence can be called during discussions that have become too heated. Hawaiian council leaders declare cooling-off periods of silence, called *ho'omalu*, that give members time to reflect on the purpose of the process and bring their emotions under control. Quakers also call for periods of silent worship when a meeting is getting out of hand. Sometimes the meeting is halted altogether, with an agreement to reconvene in a month. Here, too, the break provides time to reflect and to heed the voice of inner wisdom.

The many inflections of silence are integral to the group voice. Silence can be pointed—when people refuse to respond to an outrageous comment, for example. It can be respectful, as when a long pause follows a particularly moving statement. It can indicate accord, pleasure, surprise, and depth of feeling, as well as sarcasm, humor, hostility, and punishment. But most importantly, silence gives people permission to speak thoughtfully and sincerely. When a speaker remains silent for a time, it indicates that he or she is waiting for the right moment or idea, not choosing words hastily. In council, each speaker is expected to pause before beginning, waiting for inner truth to reveal itself. Willingness to listen deeply makes the passing of the talking stick more than simply an exotic method of raising hands.

CREATIVITY SALONS: CONVERSATION AT PLAY

The poem, the song, the picture is only water drawn from the well
of the people, and it should be given back to them in a cup of beauty
so that they may drink—and in drinking, understand themselves.

~ Federico García Lorca, Spanish poet

Artistic expression has always been part of the salon experience. Queen Christina of Sweden, living in regal retirement in Rome in the seventeenth century, held a wildly popular salon at which music, dancing, and improvised theatrical performances delighted those in attendance. Not even the disapproval of the archly antitheater Pope Innocent XI could keep Christina's guests (including cardinals and bishops) from attending and taking part. At one time or another, almost every contemporary salon also turns to a creative activity, whether it's putting together a newsletter, playing charades, reading aloud, or indulging in musical free-for-alls. Many salons devote at least one annual gathering to some kind of creative group project—dabbling in clay, singing, attending concerts or theatrical performances as a group. Some salonists like to quilt while they talk, or play card games during conversation breaks.

Ronny Barkay's Los Angeles salon loves to push the envelope of activities. They discuss issues, but also go on film and museum outings, hold Oscar Night parties (with voting), exchange wrapped white elephant gifts accompanied by mysterious poems that hint at the contents, and "play" music by singing through cardboard toilet-tissue and paper-towel rolls (the "Baa-Baa Band"). A few years ago, Barkay and company even produced two "Salon On the Air" broadcasts on a public-access cable channel.

Members of a salon in California's Silicon Valley hold two monthly meetings—one for the "Silicon-versationalists" and another for "Sili-creationists." A salon in Southern California added two writers' groups, a postmodern readers' group, a general readers' group, and a political action group to its regular session. The Marharbour salon, founded by Mary Marr in Denver, is a veritable art center: It offers classical music programs, art and photography shows, poetry, and dance. A creative writing group meets on Tuesday nights, and discussion salons are held the third Wednesday of every month. Julius Sokolsky's New York salon boasts a stand-up comic as a member, and serious discussions of the role of humor in modern life can quickly turn into schtick.

Lana Turner sometimes surprises members of her Harlem salons with a writer or musician, who talks with the group and presents his or her work following dinner. "It's a nice departure, a way for people to talk to the artist," she says. "The things that become the most important are the things that are most personal. You don't get the same feeling when you leave a major concert at the Paramount theater or Radio City. You may think 'That was wonderful,' but you very rarely have a lasting sense of coming into contact with somebody. My guests hear directly about ways that someone can construct a frame or movie or script, a novel, someone who performs well, who sings."

The Washington Area Artists' Salon in drum-and-dance mode

When people make art for themselves in creativity salons, they come to understand the creative process better. They're less intimidated by, and more appreciative of, professional works of art, and more supportive of creativity in others. Ultimately, experimenting with creativity gives everyone a chance to develop abilities and the freedom to exercise them.

Creative projects can also stimulate salon discussion, especially if the activities deliver a message or adhere to a theme. On one June evening in 1991, for example, *Utne Reader* held an outdoor salon from six to midnight. Comedy, dance, and music alternated with discursive minisalons that took up topics inspired by the performances. And Nina Simons, in her annual Bioneers Conference in California, mixes cutting-edge ecological ideas presented by speakers with discussion and performances designed to heighten the mood of creativity and innovation.

ORGANIZING A CREATIVITY SALON

Starting and organizing a creativity salon can be challenging, but the rewards can also be immense. Many creative activities are noisy and supply-intensive, and work best in a large, open room. They also tend to last longer than the average discussion, so plan on setting aside at least four hours for a creativity salon, and as many as six or seven hours for some projects. Certain events, such as the Foto Safari (see the "Art Projects" section) or building a sand castle, can consume an entire day and are best conducted outdoors.

Creative activities may require initial explanation, warm-up exercises, or training, so prompt arrival is important. Once the salon begins, it should progress from structured activities to looser, more improvised ones. With musical or theatrical undertakings in particular, a structured warm-up will keep later improvisations from being pure cacophony. Start an evening of noise-music improvisation by assigning the numbers one through eight, then have the members make a noise each time their number comes up in an eight-count beat. Continue for a while before slipping into improvisational mode.

Plan a break after the first couple of hours. During the break, ask your members what they think about the project so far. Solicit suggestions for variations or rule changes.

A creativity group can be much larger than a conversational one, provided there's room for everyone. Groups of from fifteen to thirty aren't uncommon when creativity is on the agenda. This is, as you might expect, one of the easiest sorts of salons for children to join. If the activity is too difficult for them, they'll take advantage of the general atmosphere of fun to play happily by themselves.

DYNAMICS OF THE CREATIVITY PROCESS

People who do not break things first will never learn to create anything.
~ Filipino proverb

Creativity salons focus on providing an atmosphere that fosters spontaneous, uninhibited, inspired behavior. The salon leader's role is to set the stage for an experience, not to direct it. Create the setting, provide any necessary props, then let whatever happens take place without interference. Any attempt to control, organize, or time the activities is hard on spontaneity.

What a leader can do once the salon has begun is to be aware of the issues that confront participants in creative play groups. Almost everyone feels hopelessly inept in at least one area of creative endeavor. People will insist they can't sing, draw, tell jokes, or act their way out of a paper bag. You can reduce their anxieties in a number of ways. For starters, make sure there's plenty of variety in salon activities, which increases the likelihood that everyone will eventually find something that she or he is comfortable with. From time to time, choose obscure activities that are likely to be new to everybody (making glass beads, decoupage). Call on everyone for activity ideas, emphasize collaboration, and enforce the all-important no-critique rule.

THE NO-CRITIQUE RULE

Never tell anyone he has no talent. That you may not say. That you do not know. That is the one absolute prohibition.

~ Martha Graham, dancer and choreographer

As one salonist wrote on the invitation to her creativity salon, "Perfection is unnecessary. Criticism is stifling. Creativity is not a god. ART IS PLAY." The no-critique rule makes it possible for newcomers to participate freely with people they haven't met before. It helps shy people and allows those who consider themselves uncreative to play fearlessly.

Even compliments can be stifling. Approval can make a creator begin to stand outside of the creation, judging it. Natural, spontaneous creativity occurs in the absence of rewards as well as punishments. General expressions of approval, delivered subtly, can be fine. At open poetry readings, for example, there's nothing wrong with letting listeners hum or nod in satisfaction after a good poem, but it's better not to tell the poet which lines or images seemed particularly moving. Why? Because analysis instantly ruins the mood of a creative salon. When people know they will be expected to provide a critique, many stop listening deeply to the poetry and start framing their comments. Meanwhile, other writers in the group may decide not to read at all, fearing a bland or dismissive response.

COLLABORATIONS

Making every creative project a collaborative "jam session" is another way to take the pressure off individuals. With a little ingenuity, almost any creative activity can become a collaboration. You can, for example, break the isolation of writing poetry by taking turns reading poetry aloud while the group improvises dance and music to accompany the spoken words. Or have two readers read two entirely different poems aloud, each reciting a few lines at a time as though acting out two parts of a scripted dialogue. The result is likely to make a strange kind of sense and a have an unruly beauty here and there.

Or have each salonist compose a four-line poem, number the lines, cut up the poems, and pass out the newly liberated lines at random so that each person receives four unrelated lines. Have the recipients assemble the lines in whatever order they choose, alter the grammar slightly if necessary, give the new work a title, and read the poems aloud.

Even when they're working on their own, salonists can chat with one another, walk around the room to look at one another's work, ask for advice, or borrow tools. Use every opportunity to keep the salon from devolving into a collection of isolated art-makers. And note that a few people will inevitably feel disappointed with the results of their individual efforts, so it's a good idea to schedule an interactive group project for your next session.

CHOOSING PROJECTS

Unless your group is determined to limit itself to one kind of artistic activity, variety is of the essence in choosing creative projects. In most cases, avoid repeating activities. The point of a creativity salon isn't to perfect your skills in a particular art form but to play with different media, tools, and techniques, and in so doing become less inhibited. Although your meeting space will limit your artmaking options to some degree—it's hard to fling paint around with abandon in a posh apartment— you can make most spaces work with a little effort and plastic tarps, newspapers, and cloths. Cover everything carefully, gather your messes in the tarps and cloths when you're done, and you can leave the most pristine place in pristine condition.

The key is not to limit yourself to narrow definitions of what's "creative" or "artistic." Creativity lies in the process and the attitude, not in the outcome.

The simplest way to decide what to do at each meeting is to throw the question open to everyone in the salon. The skills and hobbies of members can become terrific group projects.

If you'd like to be more systematic, even classical, in your approach, try scheduling activities according to each of the nine Greek Muses: Calliope (epic poetry), Euterpe (music and lyric poetry), Erato (love poetry), Polyhymnia (sacred poetry), Clio (history), Melpomene (tragedy), Thalia (comedy), Terpsichore (dance), and Urania (astronomy). Or you might take the psychological approach, choosing activities that will stimulate each of five types of intelligence: bodily/kinesthetic, musical, linguistic/verbal, visual/spatial, and logical/mathematical. Collaborations of all sorts, particularly theatrical games, help develop interpersonal intelligence.

Or choose a theme, then come up with as many activities as possible that are connected to it. Your salon might carry the idea of architecture through several sessions: building fanciful buildings out of cardboard or Styrofoam, reading or composing poems about architecture and famous buildings, drawing floor plans of childhood homes from memory, visiting notable works of architecture in your city and photographing or writing about the experience in offbeat ways.

The key is not to limit yourself to narrow definitions of what's "creative" or "artistic." A visit to any modern art museum will show you that almost anything can be considered art, from Marcel Duchamp's famous urinal-as-sculpture to Ad Reinhardt's all-black paintings. Creativity lies in the process and the attitude, not in the outcome.

LANGUAGE GAMES

All was done gaily and without grimaces. No one bit his fingernails, and no one stopped laughing or speaking. All that was heard were challenges and answers, assaults and the return sallies.

~ Madeleine de Scudéry, describing rhyming games in her salon

Language games are the least messy, the least expensive, and the least physical of creative projects. They run the gamut from witty remarks uttered in the ephemeral flow of salon conversation to verbal performances—recitations, improvisations, readings, plays—to poems and stories recorded on paper. Enjoyable in themselves, linguistic games also help to improve conversation by giving salonists a license to joke, rhyme, coin epigrams, and generally behave like witty salon habitués of the highly verbal eighteenth century.

Verbal play can be as simple as reading aloud from favorite books of poetry and prose. (This can evolve into group performances, with others playing music or acting out the texts.) It can be as salon-traditional as writing one- or two-line poems or epigrams on set topics and reading them aloud. One of the liveliest word games is the coining of "venereal nouns." The word doesn't refer to a sexually transmitted disease, but to collective nouns for animals (from Latin *venare*, to hunt). "A pride of lions" or "an exaltation of larks" are traditional examples, but you can extend venereal nouns beyond the animal kingdom. How about "a flush of plumbers," "a sprawl of malls," "a rack of sadomasochists"?

Verbal games invented by André Breton and his surrealist associates in Paris in the 1920s have lost none of their ability to surprise and delight. The most famous of these is The Exquisite Corpse. Start it by writing an article (*the, a*) and an adjective on a piece of paper. Fold the paper so the words can't be seen, and pass it along. The next person writes a noun, folds the paper, and passes it. The game continues with a verb, another article and adjective, and another noun or noun phrase. During a rather quiet, humdrum gathering of surrealists in 1925, poet Jacques Prévert invented the game by scribbling "The exquisite corpse" on a piece of paper and passing it. "Shall drink," "the new," and "wine" followed as the paper made the rounds. Writing in 1968, André Breton's first wife, Simone Collinet, described the effect of the game on its inventors:

> Once their imagination was let loose, it couldn't be stopped. André exclaimed with delight and immediately saw in it one of those wellsprings or natural outpourings of inspiration he so loved to discover. A torrent was unleashed. . . .Violent surprises prompted admiration, laughter, and stirred an unquenchable craving for new images—images inconceivable to one brain alone—born from the involuntary, unconscious, and unpredictable mixing of three or four heterogeneous minds.

This game and many others are beautifully described in the Surrealist Games box, available in many game shops and bookstores.

And before you leave the game shop/bookstore, look around for other ideas. Many games now on the market, such as Pictionary, Fictionary, and Password, were adapted from simple parlor games that originally required nothing more than pen and paper. You may be able to play them without buying the packaged versions. And the many books on verbal creativity on your bookstore's Writing Aids and Self-Help shelves are packed with ideas for you to adopt and adapt.

PERFORMANCE AND IMPROVISATION

If you can walk, you can dance. If you can talk, you can sing.
~ Proverb from Zimbabwe

Performance activities—including music, singing, dance, and theatrical games—are the most physical, ephemeral, and exuberant of creative projects. Although it can be great fun for one group of salon members to entertain the others, in many performance games the participants are artist and audience at the same time. That's the case with the potluck dinner at which guests are not allowed to feed themselves, but have to wait to be fed by others. Or guests can bring finger foods and eat blindfolded. At one Minnesota salon, members brought food that had emotional significance for them and shared it with the group, along with stories and memories of the food. And you can make music without a single traditional instrument: Beans in glass jars, springs, wine glasses with water in them, sticks, pots, voices, and hand claps can make an amazing orchestra.

The Color Transformations game can transform a standard discussion salon. The whole group comes dressed in one color from head to toe, and during a break changes into another head-to-toe outfit of a contrasting color. Watch how the color shift affects the mood of the group.

From stylized tableaus to uninhibited comic improvisation, theater games have been central to salons throughout history, and one of the most consistently popular has been charades. If your group tires of the familiar American form of the game—in which people act out the words or syllables of a familiar phrase, and which, tradition says, originated when the Algonquin Round Table altered the rules of English charades—try the game in its very earliest form, *tableaux vivants*. Break the group into teams of four or five people. Have each group decide on a famous painting or sculpture, or a scene from a well-known movie, book, commercial, or billboard advertisement. Using props if necessary, each team strikes a pose that recreates the scene, and everyone else tries to guess what they're portraying.

In another early version of charades, players divided a name into syllables and told a riddle for each one. In his excellent historical study of charades, word-lore expert James Charlton offers the following example:

My first is a part of the face;
My second is a kind of jam;
My third is a pleasure boat;
My whole is a well-known English authoress.
The answer: Jaw-jelly-yacht, or George Eliot.

ART PROJECTS

At one salon we made gift wrap. I wrote on it one of my favorite quotes by Brenda Ueland, about not grinding when you're trying to be creative and just letting it flow out of you. I have it up on my wall and . . . I look at it and think about the night I made it. Those were great times.

~ Judy Bell, member of the Loring Cafe Salon

Art projects are usually easy to think up, but a bit of work to bring off. You may need some extra space, better light, more ventilation, or noise-proofing. Art supplies need to be bought (take up a collection for this) or brought from home by all. To find project ideas, visit art stores and peruse craft and activity books for children (this is play, after all). For more sophisticated ideas and inspirations, nothing works better than a group visit to a museum of contemporary art.

Use simple, strong themes to set members thinking. Activist Joanna Macy suggests making "collages for a peaceful world." Pose the question "What would a world of peace and justice look like?" and collage the answer, with all imaginable materials. You might dye eggs Ukrainian style around Easter, make masks around Halloween, or create gift wrap at the winter solstice, with butcher-block paper, cheap fabric, and any adornments at all, from paint to paste-on collage pieces.

The Foto Safari moves your salon outdoors, usually for half a day, so you may want to schedule it for a Saturday or Sunday morning and hope for cooperative weather. Before the session, prepare a list of short, punchy phrases, sentences, and quotes. Comedic or offbeat sentences that lend themselves to several interpretations are best. (Television and advertising are good places to glean these.) You should have one or two pages full of phrases, photocopied so that each participant has a copy of the list. Ask people to bring cameras and film. When they arrive, split your salon into groups of three or four, with one camera per group. Then have the groups go for a walk and take pictures, keeping the list of phrases in mind as captions for their pictures. (Posing and using props are allowed.) Shoot a roll of film, have it developed at a one-hour film processing place, and reconvene. When the photos are mounted next to the captions they illustrate, be prepared to laugh, and to marvel at the ways in which your groups interpreted the captions.

The study circle, council, and creativity approaches can be applied to your salon to any degree you choose. You can adopt any of them outright as your format, or experiment with them from time to time. Study circles move your salon out into engagement with the world, council tends to move the salon and its members inward, and creativity operates where art does: back and forth across the boundary between the self and the world. All three modes intensify the salon process by going beyond talk into other realms of experience—action, contemplation, creation.

CHAPTER TEN

BOOK CLUBS

We meet twice weekly to discuss the nuances and ideals, interests and ideas, thoughts and metaphors, history and hearsay, truths and standards, relevancy and subjectivity, of and around that week's reading. Basically, twenty people sit and talk about life in relation to the Iliad *or the* Bible.

~ Rachel Nesse, book club member

Though book clubs and salons share many characteristics, the book club has a distinguished history of its own, quite distinct from that of the salon. While many of the writers who attended the classic salons were in no way shy about reading their work to the assembled group (Molière at the Hôtel de Rambouillet, the popular novelist Marmontel at Julie de Lespinasse's soirees), attendees at a given salon rarely prepared themselves for conversation by reading the same book beforehand—the hallmark of the book club.

The book club proper could be said to have begun, at least in America, with the religious renegade Anne Hutchinson, on her way to the Massachusetts Bay Colony in 1634. Hutchinson gathered a group of women on board a Massachusetts-bound ship to do something women were not encouraged to do in Puritan culture: discuss the sermon preached at the Sunday shipboard service. When they arrived in the Bay Colony, she continued these all-female discussion groups. Needless to say, the idea of a group of women talking over religious issues without male guidance (that is, dominance) did not sit well with the authorities in the Puritan colony. The gatherings were condemned by the colony's general assembly "as a thing not tolerable nor comely in the sight of God nor fitting for your sex."

While this was not a book club in the strict sense—call it a "sermon club"—it inaugurated a tradition of serious discussion of serious texts by women. It grew out of Hutchinson's belief that interior, personal religious intuition and conviction were more important than observance of external forms, a notion that soon got her banished from Massachusetts

Anne Hutchinson preaching

altogether. (She became one of the first settlers of Rhode Island.) But a connection between book clubs and free thought and action—particularly female free thought and action—had been established.

Admittedly, the book clubs that followed were a bit tame. In the early nineteenth century, "mite" or "cent" societies formed: women contributed one cent a week to sewing/reading circles for the purchase of edifying religious literature, which they discussed under strict male clerical supervision. After the Civil War, however, secular women's book clubs grew like wildfire, tackling issues of increasing political and social seriousness. In their living rooms, women read, discussed, and presented papers on literature, art, science, and politics. At a time when only a handful of colleges and universities accepted female students, these literary societies, so often named after a Muse or a Greek philosopher, ended up being the oratorical and intellectual training grounds for the women who would lead the movement for suffrage and other rights for women.

The other major ancestor of the modern book club is the Great Books movement. In 1929, Robert Maynard Hutchins took over as president of the University of Chicago, instituting a core curriculum based on a canon of famous Western books, which Hutchins himself and the philosopher Mortimer J. Adler taught seminar-style and introduced at various levels of the university.

In an age dominated by galloping technology and specialized vocational training, Hutchins' humanistic insistence that the close reading of philosophy and literature should be the foundation of education found a surprisingly willing audience outside the university as well. Various adult education systems and private study groups adopted the Hutchins-Adler list of Great Books for reading and discussion, and in 1952, *Great Books of the Western World* was published as a fifty-four-volume shelf of reading, from Homer to Machiavelli to Freud—a classic framing of the "dead white male" canon. By the end of the 1950s some 50,000 readers were registered with the Great Books program, and countless others were probably following it in whole or in part. (The program still has 20,000 enrollees in some 1,800 groups around the country.)

Today we are in the midst of a huge renaissance of book clubs. Rachel Jacobsohn, author of *The Reading Group Handbook*, estimates that the number of reading groups in the United States has more than doubled since 1994, for a total of something like half a million—and Jacobsohn says that's a conservative estimate. According to Virginia Valentine, book group coordinator for Denver's Tattered Cover bookstores, book clubs are still mainly female. And the preferred reading matter is overwhelmingly fiction—and mostly literary fiction. "*Cold Mountain, Memoirs of a Geisha*, but not the offbeat stuff," according to Valentine. "These women are well-educated, with jobs and family. Half of them, at least half of those I deal with, are living in the suburbs, where there is a sense of isolation. For these women, book clubs are a natural way of getting together."

Such generalizations have exceptions, of course. The Gay Men's Book Group of Ridgefield, Connecticut, has read James Baldwin's *Giovanni's Room*, E.M. Forster's *Maurice*, and a number of nonfiction titles about gay life. Toronto's Quill and Swill group was started, according to the group's statement of purpose, "with the goal of recreating those late-night, booze-fueled, rambling philosophical discussions that used to erupt frequently at University, only with better food. As a result, unlike [in] many book circles, there is no formal 'policy' on what we read; historically the emphasis has been on recent fiction by Canadian authors but we deviate wildly from that quite frequently."

One of the more sensational developments in the book club culture has been Oprah Winfrey's involvement. When the queen of daytime television announced in September 1996 that she was starting an on-the-air book club and the first book to be discussed would be Jacquelyn Mitchard's *The Deep End of the Ocean*, the

> **T**oronto's Quill and Swill book group was started, according to the group's statement of purpose, "with the goal of recreating those late-night, booze-fueled, rambling philosophical discussions that used to erupt frequently at University, only with better food."

New York Public Library got 4,000 requests for the book. This literary novel by a far-from-famous writer eventually sold 3 million copies, running well ahead of Stephen King and Sue Grafton on *The New York Times* best-seller list for weeks.

These numbers got the attention of the book trade. When Winfrey announced her second selection, Toni Morrison's 1977 novel, *Song of Solomon*, 730,000 new paperback copies were immediately issued (only 360,000 had been released in the previous nine years). On the day of the announcement alone, Barnes & Noble sold 16,070 copies. *Time* magazine noted that Oprah boosted Morrison's commercial clout more than the 1993 Nobel Prize in literature did.

Amid the hype, it's easy to ignore what Winfrey is actually accomplishing with her on-air book club and book-talk conferences on the Oprah Web site. "I've always loved books," she told *Time*. "When I was growing up in Mississippi and Nashville, that's all I had. My idea is to reintroduce reading to people who've forgotten it exists." Winfrey has broken the book-club mold by attracting blue-collar women, including many women of color. Winfrey selects books like *Breath, Eyes, Memory* by Edwidge Danticat, *I Know This Much Is True* by Wally Lamb, and *Tara Road* by Maeve Binchy—plot-driven books that tend to highlight adversity overcome by plucky, usually female, main characters with whom a reader can easily identify. While not experimental, the books are ambitious and challenging works of literature that provide windows into a variety of worlds and perspectives.

Publishers, bookstores, and libraries have never been more conscious of book groups and helpful to them. In short, there's never been a better time to join or start one.

STARTING OR JOINING A BOOK CLUB: RESOURCES

Looking for a book club to join? It might work best to start your own. Existing clubs that want to admit new members are few and far between (book clubs are, as a rule, cohesive and long-lived), and given the amount of institutional help out there for starting one, it may indeed be your best bet. Gather four or five like-minded friends. If you're lucky enough to live in a city with a large, full-service independent bookstore like Denver's Tattered Cover, Elliott Bay in Seattle, or Books & Books in Miami, you can bring the group to meet with book-club advisers on the store's staff or consult by phone. The staff members will tell you what the store can do for your group. They might be able to provide meeting space, written reviews of or brief presentations on books your group is likely to want to read and discuss, and advice about how to make book groups work. All on the understanding, of course, that the group will buy its books from the store.

Virginia Valentine of Tattered Cover mentors some four hundred book groups in the Denver area and across the nation. And she sticks with them past the start-up phase, providing ongoing advice when they need revitalization or want to make major changes. At Books & Books in Miami, book club coordinator Colleen Hettich helps out six groups

The LoDo (Lower Downtown Denver) Book Group

that meet in the store, and twenty groups that have agreed to make Books & Books their supplier. She arranged for one book club to meet over coffee with novelist Susan Minot, who was reading at the store.

If you're not able to take advantage of services like these, there are still plenty of resources you can use to get going. Books like *The New York Public Library Guide to Reading Groups* by Rollene Saal, *The Book Group Book* by Ellen Slezak, *The Reading Group Book* by Holly Hughes and David Laskin, and Rachel Jacobsohn's *Reading Group Handbook* all offer tips on getting up and running, troubleshooting ideas, and case histories of successful groups. Many public libraries also offer advice and support for book clubs, including reading lists.

WHAT TO READ?

No matter how much help you get, the success of a book group, like that of a salon, is ultimately in your hands. Many of the points made in this book about salon organization and leadership apply to book groups as well. It pays, for example, to be clear about your goals for the group: Are you a serious book-study circle, or are the books intended as jumping-off places for sociability? Are you going to read mainly fiction, nonfiction, poetry, plays—or a bit of everything?

The big difference between salons and book clubs, of course, is that the group's conversation revolves around books, which provide the pretext and the focal point for discussion. This is a big advantage, but it brings with it a problem: deciding what to read.

First, you need ideas. Bookstore and library browsing will turn up many possible titles, or you can "shop" in list books like *What to Read: The Essential Guide for Reading Group Members and Other Book Lovers* by Mickey Pearlman, *500 Great Books by Women* by Jesse Larson, Erica Bauermeister, and Holly Smith, or (for the dead-white-male-minded) *The Western Canon* by Harold Bloom. Or visit one of the online indexes to book reviews, like BookWire (www.bookwire.com) or Booklist (www.ala.org/booklist). Librarians and bookstore folk also will be eager to make suggestions.

Next comes selecting books. You can leave that up to a different group member each meeting; the person who selects a book typically acts as discussion leader and facilitator when you talk about it. You can vote on suggestions. You can decide in that tried-and-true salon manner, consensus—discussing until everybody, or nearly everybody, is nodding their heads. Or you can do what Karen Ackland's Santa Cruz, California, group does: decide on a meal first, and pick a book to go with it (Egyptian lamb stew suggested Egyptian novelist Naguib Mahfouz; with an English-style outdoor tea, Kazuo Ishiguro's *The Remains of the Day*). Some groups don't select a book unless at least one member has read it already.

Two important details: Choose books three months in advance, to allow plenty of time for acquiring and reading it. And consider holding off on brand-new books until paperbacks come out—it's easier on the pocketbook.

Finally, there's acceptance. Everybody needs to be prepared to compromise on book selection, and expect to read outside their areas of interest or expertise. That's a salon tradition: stretching the self. Don't be alarmed if one or two members drop out over the choice of reading material. You're better off without the disgruntled.

WHAT'S A GOOD BOOK CLUB BOOK?

There's a reason why so many book club books are "literary" fiction, that is, fictional writing that engages serious and resonant ideas while telling a good story with believable characters. The fact is, genre fiction—mysteries, romances, stolen-submarine thrillers, and some science fiction—generally doesn't work well for discussion groups. That's not because genre literature isn't enjoyable to read and often well-crafted; the books are simply so plot-driven and explicit about everything from the hero's stony jaw to the evil of the renegade plutonium thief that there's not very much to talk about. Good literary fiction leaves a lot unsaid. Resonances, implications, ambitious themes subtly touched upon—all are good for chewing on and talking over. (For an even more intense experience of the unsaid and implied, try poetry.)

Nonfiction may appeal to the group mainly for its subject matter, but take care to select works that are as well and interestingly

> **G**enre fiction generally doesn't work for discussion groups. The books are simply so plot-driven and explicit about everything from the hero's stony jaw to the evil of the renegade plutonium thief that there's not very much to talk about.

written as good fiction. That way you'll be able to talk about the book, not just the subjects or ideas in the book. You'll find it easier to pay fruitful attention to the how as well as the what: how the author sees and shapes her material, what captures her imagination, how her choices of what to say and what to leave unsaid shape your response to the subject, whether it's the Civil War or synergy.

BOOK CLUB READING: THE QUESTIONER'S PATH

Your group may decide to draft a list of discussion questions applicable to every book. By asking them as you read, you prepare for discussion. Whether or not your group does this, though, questions are your way into the book. In How to Read a Book, philosopher and Great Books promoter Mortimer Adler proposes three basic questions any reader can ask: What is the author saying? What does he or she mean? How true is it? Elliott Bay's Web site suggests the following more detailed list:

- What aspects of the main character do you admire or distrust?
- What are the significant interactions among the characters?
- What are their distinguishing characteristics?
- What makes the minor characters memorable?
- What scenes reveal the most about characters' underlying purposes and motives?
- What is the book's theme?
- Is there underlying symbolism?
- Does the book seem autobiographical?
- How do the time and place affect the book overall?
- What are the social (racial, gender) implications of the story?
- What do you think is the climax of the book?
- By the end, has the book dealt satisfactorily with all the issues it has brought up?
- What kind of emotional response do you think the author was trying to evoke in the reader?
- What other titles might you have given the book?

Here are a few even subtler questions:

- How much control did a given character have over his or her actions?
- How did the narrative form of the book—the way the author chose to tell the story—contribute to its success or failure?
- How did the author's or characters' point of view affect the story?
- How did language, diction, sentence structure, and syntax contribute to the book?
- What part did present, past, and future time play in the story?

As you read, take notes. Have small Post-it notes at hand to mark places in the book that support your answers to these questions and any others that you and the group generate.

THE DREADED R-WORD: RESEARCH

If book groups are supposed to be life-enhancing, and they are, then how can we even suggest that members engage in *research*, that dreary throwback to college days? The truth is that research truly is life-enhancing when it comes to book-group discussion. It could even make or break your group.

Why? Because the extra knowledge, color, and context supplied by research nourishes the group, connects the book to people's lives, and thus quite literally gives everyone more to talk about. More talk, especially more talk on concrete questions brought up by research, means a more vigorous, long-lived book club.

Twenty minutes spent with a librarian, particularly one in the research library of a major university—if you have one nearby—can familiarize you with the basic tools of literary research, from compilations of author biographies and book reviews to online indexes of periodicals. Articles in scholarly journals can, and in the case of major authors often do, focus on practically anything in a given novel or body of novels: water-plant imagery, images of motherhood, Old Testament allusions, references to popular culture, and so on.

Interviews with authors are particularly useful to book groups. They're a natural and vivacious way into the mind of the writer, and their unpredictability contrasts nicely with the plodding, meet-every-objection style of much academic writing. Collecting reviews of the volume under discussion not only provides a number of perspectives, but also shows the peccadilloes and prejudices of reviewers in a particularly clear light— good training for book group discussion.

You might assign one person to provide research materials on each book you discuss. Some groups like to go en masse to the library and renew their research skills with the aid of a librarian.

BOOK CLUB DISCUSSION: ON TRACK OR OFF?

The normal rules of the road for salon conversation apply to book discussion, with the added issue of whether (and how) to stay on task—that is, to keep talking about the book. " 'We got off the track' is one of the commonest complaints I hear from book groups," says Tattered Cover's Virginia Valentine. A decision about the group's primary purpose needs to be made up front, and, if that purpose is talking about the book, the facilitator needs to tactfully remind and re-remind the group when talk swerves away from the book and into personal reminiscences spurred by the writing, free-associative riffs, or social chatter. Set aside time for socializing at the beginning or end of the evening.

Interestingly enough, research is a formidable tool in helping book clubbers stay on track. Groups that do outside research tend to have the most satisfying meetings, enriched by new content and fresh perspectives. In other words, a context-rich discussion is so interesting that nobody wants to "escape."

BEYOND BOOKS: ADDED BOOK CLUB ATTRACTIONS

Just like salons, book clubs can be inventive in the ways that they stretch and augment their discussions with special events and offbeat experiences. The Friends of the Library Book Club in Seattle invites university scholars to address their club when they read Dickens. Another group, to underscore the theme of cannibalism in two books on their agenda, *Lord of the Flies* and *John Dollar*, served gingerbread men, lustily biting off the helpless little limbs. The Lit Group in suburban Detroit became so entranced with Nien Cheng's harrowing memoir *Life and Death in Shanghai* that founding members Audrey Kron and Edie Broida called on the author at her home in Washington, D.C. The bond that resulted has grown so close that Cheng has met all the members of the group, and Kron calls Cheng every Mother's Day.

Other ideas: Select books for discussion based on the schedule of authors' visits to a local bookstore or college, then make a point of meeting the writers. Rent films based on the books you discuss and compare print with celluloid. Choose books set in your city or region and visit the scenes of the action. In short, be as imaginative in your savoring of books as their authors were in creating them.

CHAPTER ELEVEN

ONLINE SALONS

As we hope you've seen by now, there are countless good reasons for starting or joining salons. But they're not for everyone. Maybe you find the thought of participating in an ongoing discussion group daunting or impossible because, for instance, you have a speech or language impediment; or because you're housebound, have a disability, or live in a remote area. Maybe you're just shy. Perhaps you can't imagine taking a couple of hours out of your busy week just to talk. Or perhaps, having arrived at a salon, you find the pressure to have a great conversation— right here and right now—oppressive. Maybe you do participate in salons, but you've found that there are some subjects—race, sex, money, intimate wishes and dreams—you don't feel comfortable talking about in a face-to-face setting. Maybe you can't find a group of people in your area with whom you would feel comfortable discussing anything. Or maybe you love saloning but are interested in expanding on the form.

Whatever the reason, if you wish for the kind of free-flowing verbal exchange described elsewhere in this book but just can't make the salon scene, there is another option: the online salon.

Granted, many people find that the brave new communications technologies—from the cell phone to the laptop-with-modem—that allow us to "keep in touch" from plane, train, automobile, and cybercafé actually prevent us from ever really talking with one another. But remarkably, as Internet critic Steven Johnson notes in his book *Interface Culture: How New Technology Transforms the Way We Create and Communicate,* the Web browser—that piece of (usually free) software that provides access to the World Wide Web from your personal computer—"turns out to be the first major technology of the twentieth century that brings strangers closer together rather than pushing them farther apart." Despite its much-talked-about shortcomings, for

The Web browser turns out to be the first major technology of the twentieth century that brings strangers closer together rather than pushing them farther apart.

those of us looking to participate in a salonlike discussion community without going face-to-face ("f2f," in online-speak), the world of computer-mediated communication has much to offer.

Although it's unlikely that you'll be able to share a plate of homemade cookies this way, or get to drive through an unfamiliar neighborhood, online salons do enjoy several advantages over the f2f kind. For one thing, the Internet's ability to gather like-minded people together is nothing less than astonishing. No matter what it is you want to discuss, you're guaranteed to find someone — perhaps someone from another country, or someone you'd never have imagined talking to in RL (online-speak for "real life") — who wants to talk about the same thing. And although many people find the lack of "presence" an obstacle to reaching the highest levels of communication, others find just the opposite. After all, communicating online usually has fewer repercussions than face-to-face conversation with people you see regularly. As a result, you may feel free to discuss things in more depth, and to reveal attitudes and experiences you might otherwise keep private. (There's such a thing as feeling too free in online discussions, of course; that topic will be covered later.)

Café Utne's homepage

Another big advantage of online salons is the ability to engage in asynchronous conversation. Time — and, therefore, geographical distance — are rendered irrelevant by what's called "bulletin board" software (because you can "post" your messages for all to read), which is the cornerstone technology of most online discussion communities. Bulletin board technology allows users to read and respond to one another's "posts" whenever they find it convenient to do so. So if you can't imagine devoting a large block of time to a salon in somebody's living room, you can always pop in to an online salon just to see what's going on. You can post a comment or two and leave, you can just "lurk" (read posts without posting), or you can stay — if you're in the mood — for hours. And, as an added benefit, the absence of time pressure allows you to think more deeply about what's been "said" (although these are written conversations, one experiences them as talking—with an added sense of publication, since there may be an audience of tens of thousands of people) and to compose your response more carefully. Add to all of these advantages the fact that complete records of every conversation usually are preserved for a week or more—which allows latecomers and newcomers to catch up before jumping in—and you can begin to see why there might be something to this online thing after all.

JOINING THE CYBERDANCE:
ONLINE SALONS AND THE SALON TRADITION

Maybe you've gone online and participated in a Usenet "thread" or someone's personal "guest book" or a public "chat" on a topic of interest to you, but quickly got tired of the repetitive and sometimes abusive exchanges so common in those forums. If so, you probably can't believe that a book about salons is encouraging people to go online. Before we talk about how to participate in or start an online salon, then, let's remind ourselves of the definition of "salon." As described elsewhere in this book, a salon—like a book club, political debate, or study circle—is a form of organized conversation between people who interact regularly.

Unlike the participants in these other forms of verbal exchange, however, a salon's members are bound together not so much by a shared interest in a particular topic as by a shared interest in the art of conversation itself. Their conversation isn't about winning or losing an argument, or sharing information on a given subject, or meeting new people, or becoming intimate with a close-knit group—though all of these things can and do happen in salons. Salon members practice conversation as an art form whose aesthetic qualities are listening well and speaking elegantly but simply. They want to inspire and be inspired, to challenge and be challenged, to amaze and be amazed.

Like an f2f salon, then, an online salon is a general conversation of an ongoing community of "users"—as those who use any kind of software online are called—that demands from each participant his or her full attention, but also intuition and imagination. The best metaphor for salonlike conversation is—as you'll hear longtime members of online communities say again and again—not a race to the finish line, but a dance. That's why posts in an online salon, like comments in an f2f salon, are less likely to be examples of defensive posturing than they are to be seductively full of poetry, nuance, emotion, and humor. Simply by joining an online salon, participants trustingly declare themselves willing to become engaged, changed, startled by new ideas and new ways of expressing old ideas. At their best, online salons offer what one guest at Rahel Levin's salon described as "the boldest ideas, the deepest thoughts, the cleverest witticisms, the most capricious fancies, all strung together by careless chit-chat."

Online salons are becoming easier to access and use with each passing month: There are more Web forums, easier tools, and clearer implementation. Many conference systems are beginning to bridge the gap between "live" chats and asynchronous conferencing by integrating instant messaging—so you can see who's using the conference at the same time you are and have a real-time discussion. Users who appreciate the messages posted by another user can then contact that person directly and enjoy the relative intimacy that real-time communication supports. Remember, though: An online salon is not simply a disembodied version, or a parody, of a "real" salon. Although online salonists go to great lengths to replicate some of the conditions of an f2f salon—typing in descriptions of their facial expressions, for example—you are in a new and different medium here, and it has many of its own norms and mores.

A FUNNY THING HAPPENED ON THE WAY TO THE FORUM: FINDING AN ONLINE SALON

The online salon has been made possible by computer-mediated communication technology, but not all computer-mediated communications are created equal. Chat, for example, is a popular form of online communication because its real-time format is lively and engaging. Since exchanges tend to be short (no more than one or two lines of text per person), chat is primarily a means of socializing and is not well suited to in-depth, deliberative discussions. Usenet newsgroups, which are single-topic discussion forums, are also extremely popular; there are thousands of them on the Internet. But newsgroups fail to meet the aesthetic criteria of online saloning: They're focused on exchange of information, and they lack a sense of play and open-endedness.

Internet mailing lists ("listservs"), in which users subscribe to a common list, and in which a posting (via e-mail) to that list is "served," by a host computer, to all users simultaneously, comes close to allowing the salon experience. E-mail's main advantage is that it's a "push" technology—you don't have to go to a Web site and check to see if there are new posts in your salon. But listserv e-mail comes into your in box along with everything else—work-related mail, personal mail, and junk mail—with the result that, even if you filter it into its own mailbox, you inevitably begin to feel that mail from your listserv group is just that: mail. It's difficult to maintain the illusion, when you're participating in listserv-type "discussion," that you're sharing a time and space with the other members of your group.

What's the answer, then? Consider online "conferencing systems" (also known as "message boards" and "Web forums"), which are made possible by bulletin board technology, hosted by a single host computer, accessible via a Web browser. In an online conference, you can post whatever it is you have to say, for all to read, and others can post replies. Unlike a real-life bulletin board, which tends to get chaotic after a while, an online bulletin board allows its users to organize their posts neatly into topics, or discussion "threads." A Web conference, or forum, is simply a collection of threads. Within threads, each of which is devoted to a particular topic, participants read and post. So if, for example, I'm burning to talk about Russia's economic crisis, I can go to an international politics-oriented Web site that supports various discussion communities, click on the "Russia" conference, then choose the "Economic crisis" thread from among the many discussions within that folder. After I read what's been posted in that thread, if the tenor and level of the conversation suits me, I am free to join in the fun. It's as simple as that.

It's so simple, in fact, that participating in discussion communities is one of the most popular online activities; even as you read this page, thousands of people all over the world are online, sharing their thoughts and feelings on every subject imaginable. Some of them are even participating in online salons.

The best way to get a good idea of how bulletin boards work, and to see how you can have a truly salonlike experience using bulletin board technology, is to sample existing Web forums. ForumOne calls itself "the Web's search engine for online forums" (www.ForumOne.com/). Its free search engine allows you to search more than 300,000 Web forum discussions by subject. It also offers free information resources that help you learn more about design and management of online communities. It lists organizations that provide hosting services; it helps you register your own forum so other people can find it; and it recommends the best conferences on topics such as business, entertainment, parenting, and the arts. ForumOne even offers a free monthly newsletter reporting the latest events and trends in online communities.

Because location matters, try out a conference that's part of a "content-oriented" Web site. Just as it makes a big difference whether you hold your salon at someone's house, at a coffee shop, or at a public library, there's no comparison between a free-floating bulletin board system and one that's attached to a site about something specific. Salon, for example, is a site about culture and current affairs—a kind of New Yorker of the Web. Even though the hundreds of conversations going on in Salon's Table Talk conference area often have little or nothing to do with what's actually being published on the site, everything that brings you to a particular conference serves as some sort of filter. That is to say, people who join the Salon online community may or may not read or enjoy Salon, but they do want to be a part of a community of people who are interested in Salon.

But even at a site with a name like Salon, an online salon isn't something that you find so much as something that you make. Within each conference, or topic area, in Table Talk, there are usually anywhere from 50 to 150 ongoing discussions; each of them is a unique discussion community. Cliff Figallo, one of the founding members of the WELL (the preeminent online community since time out of mind) back in 1985, is the former director of Salon Communities, which includes both the WELL and Table Talk. Table Talk's discussion areas cover the waterfront, from the arts to business and work life, and from social issues to the imagination. Whether you want to discuss sculpture, your career, race and class, or current events—or maybe tell stories and engage in role-playing activities—there's something here for everyone.

RULES OF THE ROAD

Online salons are in some ways more fragile than f2f groups. Why? Because whereas an f2f salon has more to offer—new faces, a break from routine, a glass of wine—than just conversation, an online salon lives or dies by the quality of its exchanges. And an online salon takes place in this anonymous medium where people sometimes feel free to say whatever they want. A difference of opinion can lead to an exchange of insults, which can turn into self-perpetuating personal vendettas. These have a way of derailing conversations and consuming vast amounts of time and words in repetitive, ugly fights that are of interest to no one. That's when participants start to bail out, and getting them to come back can be very difficult. So conversation in online salons must achieve a consensus on standards of behavior that help people relax their critical or anxious scrutiny of one another and minimize friction among diverse personalities.

At most online discussion sites, you're required to read and agree to abide by the sites' terms of service. By clicking on the "I accept" button, you're usually agreeing that, for instance, you won't provide the site with false or misleading registration information, and you won't impersonate someone else. You're agreeing not to use the conference to post or distribute material (including text, graphics, video, or audio) that is unlawful, harassing, libelous, abusive, threatening, harmful, bigoted, racially offensive, obscene, or otherwise objectionable. You're agreeing not to post any form of commercial solicitation, and you're agreeing not to redistribute content posted in the conference without first getting permission from the person who posted it. It's important to obey these terms of service for two reasons. First, you can be held legally liable for what you post online. And even though these sites are easy to access, they're not public property: If site management determines that you've violated any of the guidelines, they're free to terminate your account and delete your posts, effectively ostracizing you from the community.

> **W**hereas a face-to-face salon has more to offer—new faces, a break from routine, a glass of wine—than just conversation, an online salon lives or dies by the quality of its exchanges.

How do you figure out what a particular discussion community's code of behavior is? By lurking. There are unspoken rules in every long-standing community, and you don't want to say the wrong thing. If you don't spend some time just reading posts, observing how the members of the community interact, you run the risk of barging in like a bull in a china shop. Although there's a certain amount of xenophobia out there, anyone who's willing to go through a conference system's acculturation process is usually welcomed warmly. Many established conference sites have a clearly designated area for beginners ("newbies"). This is a good place to introduce yourself, ask questions, and generally get oriented. Experienced members frequent newbie threads partly because they like to take responsibility for their community, but also to encourage promising new members to join the right threads.

NETIQUETTE: THE ART OF ONLINE POLITENESS

When you become a member of a discussion community, you're agreeing to a certain code of behavior as well as to terms of service. This code may vary wildly even within the same conference, depending on the culture of a particular thread. In general, according to Cliff Figallo, "good conversation happens between people who share the same interests and are willing to forego personal insults when disagreements arise. Our community standards are based around an ethos of mutual respect, and if someone is deliberately trying to sabotage that sense of community, we will nuke them." Here are a few pointers for posting effectively and respectfully in an online conference:

- *Compose offline:* Although posting with your modem running can be fun (since the time pressure resembles that of a real, f2f salon), it's wise to think before you speak. Especially if you're responding to a negative comment directed toward you, wait for a deeper response than your initial emotional reaction.

- *Use emotive punctuation:* One of the great drawbacks to saloning online is that you miss the elusive emotions that can sweep through an f2f group; missing, too, are those winks, squints, raised eyebrows, and hand signals that subtly halt monologues, applaud observations, lighten the mood, or signal disagreement. The "emoticon"—which uses :) (look at it side-

:-"	*pursed lips*
:-&	*tongue tied*
:-Y	*a quiet aside*
>-<	*absolutely livid*
l-)	*chortling*
:-/	*skeptical*
:-T	*trying to keep a straight face*
;-(	*crying*
{:-)	*wearing a toupee*
}:-)	*wearing a toupee in an updraft*
+O:-)	*the Pope*
%\v	*Picasso*
%-)	*has been staring at screen for 15 hours straight*

Emoticons

ways) to signal "I'm not as angry as I may sound" or ;) for "just kidding,"and so forth—can be effective. But don't overuse the signs; all that winking and nudging is cloying after a while.

- *Don't YELL:* Although it's acceptable to put a word or two in capital letters to make a POINT, people will be offended IF YOU YELL AT THEM ALL THE TIME.

- *Be brief:* Although in an f2f salon, people can jump in and interrupt, or make facial gestures at you when you've talked long enough, online you can go on and on and on and on. Maybe that's what you like to do; maybe the absence of sensory data makes you feel giddy, like you're staring into a vacuum that needs to be filled. The fact is, it's both more effective and more respectful to make your point succinctly.

- *Be clear:* Avoid vague and sweeping generalizations, use examples, tell stories, give details, make analogies, keep your language jargon-free.

- *Be tolerant of spelling and grammatical errors:* Not everyone is an experienced typist, or a great writer.

- *Be sincere:* Express your emotions honestly. Why? For one thing, without body language and tone of voice, irony and sarcasm don't translate well; people can be hurt and offended by something you meant as a joke. But sincerity is a must online for the same reason as in an f2f salon: An important part of saloning is letting your guard down, being yourself.

- *Don't "flame"* (online-speak for "make a personal attack"): Be tolerant of different ideas, of how people treat you, of idiosyncratic personalities. Above all, if you're flamed, don't respond immediately. (Cliff Figallo suggests this: "Resist the urge to flame back; log off and take a walk.") What's the difference between lively disagreement and unacceptable flaming? The universal rule of thumb is that if you find yourself name-calling, or using words and phrases you wouldn't use if the person you're addressing were in the same room with you, then you are probably over the line.

- *Argue fairly:* It's perfectly OK to argue in salons, as long as you express disagreement sincerely, and with wit and tolerance rather than rudeness, rancor, or disdain. When you argue, you reveal yourself, and you become more attentive and challenged.

- *Stay on topic:* Unless the host indicates that you're in a free-form conference topic or thread, keep your comments consistent with the stated subject. It's disrespectful to change it to something you're interested in, as though yours is the only opinion that matters. If you're not interested in a particular thread, every large conference site has dozens or hundreds more options; most will let you start your own thread, too.

HOSTING: YOUR FIRST STEPS

If you're new to the world of online salons, it might be difficult to decide: Host your salon on someone else's server (a "forum hosting service"), or use your own, or use your Internet service provider (ISP)'s server? Buy your own conferencing software or rent someone else's? And so forth. Conferencing veteran Dave R. Woolley offers—on his site, www.thinkofit.com—a comprehensive guide to software that powers discussions on the Web. He also lists dozens of free Web conferencing software products—which are generally less capable than the commercial ones.

It's smart to spend some time practicing your salon-hosting skills before taking the plunge. How can you practice? Most veterans agree that there's plenty of room for unofficial salon hosting within existing online conference systems. Even within fairly broad discussion areas— politics, art, media, sports—there's wide variation in how coherent and interesting conversations are. Often a group of people will deliberately start a discussion, and depending on how serious they are about keeping it on topic, they will claim and hold that space, or allow it to be infiltrated and diluted. So if you and, say, five to ten people you've come to know from online discussions feel ready to hold the floor, most conference systems allow you to start your own thread and run with it. It won't be private—anyone can read your posts, and jump in—but if a dedicated core group is determined to stick to its ground rules, you can demonstrate that yours is not a conversation to be trivialized or sidetracked.

THE CARE AND FEEDING OF YOUR SALON

Once you've started your own salon-within-a-conference, you'll quickly discover that keeping a good conversation going—online or off—has a mystical element. One of the great disadvantages of asynchronous conversations, for example, is that those lulls that happen in every conversation, when they occur online, may stretch out into days and even weeks. Emma Taylor, manager of NerveCenter (the community space of Nerve, a Web site dedicated to "literate smut"), and one of the founding members of a group of women-oriented Web sites called EstroNet, suggests that keeping good conversations from dying out is everyone's responsibility, but the host's job. "Being a great host doesn't mean that you always have a deep thought to express," she suggests. "Sometimes it just means being committed to keeping the place feeling lived-in, by saying 'Hey, great post!' and encouraging others to say something, anything, to keep the conversation going."

Slow times aren't the only hazard. Online salons can fail because they're too insular: People have said all they have to say to one another and need new blood to reanimate things. Or, on the other hand, online salons can fail because they're not private enough. Cliff Figallo remembers that "when *Playboy* did an article on the WELL's 'sex conference' . . . all these people suddenly showed up looking for dirty talk. These people were 'differently clued' as to what the WELL was all about, and fortunately they didn't stick around long—but it was very disruptive while it lasted, like a motorcycle gang going to a seaside resort." As a participant in a nonpublic online salon, practice welcoming newcomers to the thread. Help them figure out who's who and what's what. But also practice dealing with intrusive and abusive visitors. One of the best strategies for dealing with boors is to ignore them completely; they usually get the picture and move on.

Online salons can fail because people don't follow the rules of the road; or, conversely, because there are too many rules. As in any salon, a good host will try to strike a balance between being too active and thus stifling discussion, and being too standoffish or uninterested and allowing problems to fester. A good host is present, not necessarily intervening, just letting everyone know he or she is there. A host moves the discussion along, models good behavior, and referees when contention starts.

Finally, an online salon can fail because things get too dull. Over time, members may become so familiar with one another that their discussions become predictable. Newcomers soon pick up on the "been there, done that" vibe and find the content low key, even dull. How do you keep things lively? Emma Taylor suggests that "even though on the one hand it's the host's responsibility to keep conversations alive, it's also his or her responsibility to be aware of when a topic has run its course, and to put it out of its misery." She also suggests that hosts, when they're introducing a new topic, keep it very specific. "I've started 'feminism' topics that went nowhere, but I've started topics on a new article on feminism in *The New York Times* that have lasted for weeks."

THE ELECTRONIC LIVING ROOM:
CREATING A PRIVATE ONLINE SALON

One question: Is privacy what you really want? People join salons because they seek exposure to new ideas and contact with a broad range of people. A nice thing about the large online conference systems is that within them you can move freely from one "discussion community" to another, until you find what's right for you—at that particular moment. Still want a private salon? OK, then, read on.

The idea of starting your own discussion community from scratch is appealing in some ways. For one thing, having your own salon means you don't have to fight a preexisting conversational aesthetic, or prove yourself to a group of old-timers. So although it may take a lot of work, if you're more of a living room than a coffee shop salonist, it will be worth it. Take these final tips with you when you get your private online salon started. Good luck!

- According to Nerve's Emma Taylor, you need a core group of interesting and talkative members: "If you don't invite ten or twenty people you know and trust to help you get started, I can guarantee you won't get anywhere. However, if you're willing to do the work, and can think of people willing to start a conversation and keep it going, it can be a lot of fun." Be careful, though, about carrying off a group of people from another online salon space; they might carry a lot of baggage with them, and your brand-new salon will end up replaying old business.

- The search engine Yahoo! offers a free service called Yahoo! Clubs. You won't get a lot of walk-in traffic from neighboring discussion communities like you will at a conferencing site, but they're easy to use. You don't have to know computer language or Web design: In about five minutes, you can set up a message board and build an e-mail list to update your group with the latest news. Editing tools allow you to delete unrelated content and remove disruptive members.

- Make sure your salon has, in addition to its various topics or threads on whatever subjects you're interested in, newbie and free-form areas. An "introduce yourself" topic for newbies allows people to get a sense of who else is participating in your salon and makes it easy for you, the host, to acculturate new members. Cliff Figallo notes that "online communities want to be small, intimate enough that you know who all the members are. 'Community development' means figuring out the best way to introduce and socialize new arrivals, and the best way to familiarize newcomers with new and established customs and traditions (and with who all the players are)." A folder or conference in which free-form discussions are acceptable means that someone who doesn't find any of the existing threads appealing on a particular day need not go elsewhere in search of companionship. Emma Taylor notes that in NerveCenter's free-form "Sometimes a cigar is just a cigar" folder, people who came to talk about sex and sexuality wind up talking about the mundane details of their lives: their jobs, their pets, their families. "The funny thing is," she muses, "discussions in this folder often feel more intimate than do the ones about people's sex lives."
- Consult how-to books like *Hosting Web Communities* by Salon's Cliff Figallo and *Community Building on the Web* by Amy Joe Kim. Whether you're interested in choosing software, facilitating discussions, or generating revenue from your salon, these books have the answers.
- Delegate responsibility. If you don't, you'll never be able to take a vacation from your host duties, and if you ever decide to quit the salon, it will most likely cease to exist. Make it clear that you are the final arbiter of all disputes, but recruit loyal and responsible participants to take over or share some of your hosting responsibilities. You won't regret it!

ONLINE SALONS AND HUMAN COMMUNICATION

As online community veteran Howard Rheingold puts it, the ongoing goal of online salon culture is "civil discourse: all kinds of people having conversations and arguments about a variety of subjects and treating each other decently." On the surface, this seems an excessively modest ideal, but anyone who's ever participated in any kind of discussion community, online or off, knows how difficult it can be to achieve it.

Rheingold and other online salon hosts are evangelists of authentic conversations, from (as he puts it) "the head, the heart, and the gut." Thanks to the culture of online salons built by the dedicated effort of people like Cliff Figallo and Emma Taylor, right now thousands of men and women, from all over the world, are joining together in online discussion communities to work toward better communication, better conversations. "Interactivity" is an overused term, to be sure, but just take a look at what's happening in these conferencing systems: interaction! In a world where the "public square" seems to have been long

DAVID WARNER

abandoned, and in which too many people seem content to be pacified by their TV sets, online salonists are making contact with strangers, sharing ideas and emotions, getting to know one another and entertaining one another with witty, serious, and wild posts. And they're doing it with an ease that surpasses face-to-face saloning.

Can the culture of online salons affect the way we communicate offline, without the mediation of any so-called communications technologies? It's too early to tell, but the answer is probably yes. Just look at the lessons to be learned from saloning online. Howard Rheingold likes to warn salonists that "both civility and nastiness are contagious."

Cliff Figallo suggests that not all conflict is to be avoided; that, in fact, conflict is valuable because it tests the boundaries of your discussion community. Emma Taylor insists that you can't be passive when it comes to creating the conditions for great communication; positive effort is required on the part of all participants. These are practical pieces of wisdom that any online salonist—or any other kind of salonist, for that matter—will immediately recognize as true. When you log off the Internet and step away from your computer, there's no reason to leave that wisdom behind. There's no reason not to practice good listening skills while you're talking with someone on the street; there's no reason not to value talk for its elegance, beauty, and simplicity. There's no reason not to inspire and be inspired, to challenge and be challenged, to amaze and be amazed, everywhere you go, every day.

CHAPTER TWELVE

EXTENDED FAMILY: BUILDING COMMUNITY IN YOUR SALON

*A true community begins in the hearts of the people involved. It is not
a place of distraction, but a place of being. It is not a place where you
reform, but a place you go home to.*

~ Malidoma Patrice Somé, *Ritual: Power, Healing, and Community*

Amerian society encourages and professes to admire a certain
kind of isolation—the isolation of self-sufficiency. Yet the need for a
sense of belonging doesn't go away. In fact, if the need continues unmet
for long enough, people may experience a profound sense of loss or disturbance. Southern California psychotherapist Robert Gonzales has
noted the malaise in his clients, almost all of whom report, as he puts
it, "some form of isolation or disconnection from community." It's
hardly surprising, then, that people turn to salons not just for intellectual stimulation, but also to share their lives with their neighbors, and
thus to find a way out of isolation. They seek to belong to their neighborhoods. Whether your salon meets this need depends upon the
degree to which it functions as a community.

HALLMARKS OF COMMUNITY

One vital characteristic of community is shared time. If a community
is to be created and sustained, a majority of the members must be committed to spending time together regularly over the course of many
months or years. Shared time ensures shared experiences, which in
turn foster emotional links between people. When people spend
enough time with others in a common endeavor, they grow to love and
care about them—even if they don't see them socially or count them as
close friends. Conscious community requires that people take the time
to hash out problems as well as share conversation and good times.

Shared space is also important. Meeting repeatedly in a familiar
house or café builds a bond among your members as they come to share
a sense of "home." But even if your salon meets in varying locations,

members will perceive themselves as part of a community if they encounter each other regularly outside the salon. The neighborhood itself may become your salon's shared space.

Building community takes practice. As a group meets regularly, it develops shared history, standards of behavior, rituals and traditions. In a sense, it becomes a culture. As members come to feel part of the culture, they are likely to also become more responsible for maintaining the group. In turn, they will reap the benefits of group support. This sort of interdependence is the single most definitive feature of community. A true community is a safety net for every member, a mutual aid network made up of people and resources. Members of a group help each other find jobs, collaborate on creative efforts, swap tools, share books, attend each other's social events, watch each other's kids, help each other move, and so forth.

Individuality needs to thrive alongside interdependence, however. Community does not stand in opposition to individuality; what it opposes is anonymity, that state of soul in which people have neither community nor an internal sense of self and thus become invisible, unable to act, belonging nowhere. A healthy salon encourages individuality, tolerates eccentricity, and relishes unusual ideas. The voice of the nonconformist is welcomed as the conscience of the group, forcing people to acknowledge their preconceived notions and make decisions carefully.

> Community does not stand in opposition to individuality; what it opposes is anonymity, that state of soul in which people have neither community nor an internal sense of self and thus become invisible.

In a crucible of interdependence and individuality, disputes are bound to occur. An authentic community must have ways to mediate problems, minimizing the risk of permanent estrangement between members. The first principles of community-oriented mediation are that any problem within the group is the entire group's problem, that problems always involve more than one person, and that rarely is one person completely in the right. The idea is to resolve disputes in a manner that preserves the integrity of the group without ignoring or discounting the needs of any individual.

In that spirit, a community uses consensus, not majority rule, to make major decisions — especially those that relate to the larger world.

When your group moves beyond opposing viewpoints to a collectively acceptable answer, solution, or attitude, you are building the strongest possible bonds of community. Consensus is a decision with which all members agree. There are no majorities or minorities, no votes, and no representatives. Everyone in the group works with everyone else to form a working conclusion that all can live with. The effort to reach a decision acceptable to everyone before taking action works against the creation of factions in the group and cements solidarity.

STAGES OF COMMUNITY BUILDING

If the community is completely honest, it will remember stories not only of suffering received, but of suffering inflicted—dangerous memories, for they call the community to alter ancient evils. The communities of memory that tie us to the past also tie us toward the future as communities of hope.
~ Robert Bellah, *Habits of the Heart*

Salons that are committed to the long haul discover that new questions and problems perpetually present themselves. The structure of the salon may need continual fine-tuning as new people arrive, advocating new ideas, while founding members move away. Crises may force the group into greater intimacy than anyone might have anticipated. If your salon is to survive for more than a short time, you need to be flexible and responsive to change. It's helpful to understand the stages a typical group experiences as it struggles to establish community. Two books, M. Scott Peck's well-known *The Different Drum: Community-Making and Peace* and the comprehensive *Creating Community Anywhere* by Carolyn R. Shaffer and salonist Kristin Anundsen, lay out this process with particular clarity.

Shaffer and Anundsen refer to the initial stage of group growth as the Excitement phase, or "Getting High on Possibilities." It's the period of getting to know one another and focusing on the positive potential of the group. Because nearly everyone is polite, tolerant, and eager to make the group work, serious conflict rarely emerges during this period. Peck calls this phase of warmth and friendliness "pseudocommunity," because people do not reveal much about themselves and generally avoid disagreements. A salon made up of like-minded individuals can happily stay in this phase for years, as long as everyone is content with social conversation and no one wants to forge a deeper connection.

If you want to move your group out of this phase, encourage frankness and choose topics that evoke emotion or highlight human differences. You might address issues of class, culture, or gender, asking questions that encourage people to respond from personal experience. Your salon may discover a strong area of disagreement on its own, which will also move the group into the next stage of community building. This period of power struggles is called the Autonomy phase by Shaffer and Anundsen, while Peck labels it "chaos." Jane Mauchan described the dynamics succinctly when her e-salon entered this phase: "The polite get-to-know-you phase is over. The 'real' personalities are starting to show." This is a difficult time. Many groups break up or splinter when power struggles arise.

You'll know you've moved into this stage when members begin questioning the standards and goals of the group. Some may call for stronger leadership or rigid rules and agendas. Others may insist on dispensing with guidelines and structure altogether. At this stage, arguments are an indication that the group is heading toward greater intimacy and solidarity. All voices should be encouraged, yet facilitators must work to make sure that arguments don't devolve into name-calling. During this time, group leaders should avoid making sweeping decisions or pronouncements and instead do their best to support members' efforts to express their true feelings and ideas. Facilitators may even need to relinquish control and cease all efforts to organize or fix the group.

Peck believes that at this point the entire group needs to undergo a giving-up period, which he calls "emptiness." Members must relinquish barriers to communication, as well as expectations, prejudices, ideologies, and controlling habits that would otherwise prevent them from accepting one another. This is a painful process, but deeper friendships are the payoff for going through it. As one salonist noted, you may lose a few acquaintances along the way, but you'll gain a family.

During the Autonomy/Chaos phase, it's often helpful to shake up the established structure by trying new ways of interacting. Try some of the exercises suggested in the chapters on conversation and council, especially those designed to draw out less talkative people. Turn-taking methods, rituals, and creative games can help your members focus on the community-building process. As your group gains respect and sensitivity for each member and for the dynamics of interaction, it will move into Anundsen and Shaffer's Stability phase, or what Peck calls "community." Stability is a cheerful period in which the group is comfortable with agreed upon roles and structures. Members feel, and rightly so, that they have come through difficulties and hung together. Members have learned to trust one another. Each member has established an identity within the community.

Like other human conditions, stability is often temporary or imperfect. Your salon may occasionally lapse into its old, chaotic behavior. Old problems may resurface and have to be discussed over and over. Don't be dismayed. Healthy communities continually revisit past policies and are in a state of constant flux as the needs of community members change. It's far better to accept and move through these changes than to become rigid or intolerant of dissent.

The Creativity Salon in Berkeley, California;
coauthor Jaida n'ha Sandra in dark blouse.

If your group remains stable for some time, while maintaining enough flexibility to accommodate individual development and community evolution, it will eventually enter the phase that Anundsen and Shaffer call Synergy. Synergy is signaled by the emergence of new roles and leaders in the group, by deeper self-expression during discussions, and by a general willingness to act in ways that support and sustain the group. People trust one another, express their feelings accurately, feel safe, and are deeply committed to the group. This is a highly productive stage—a time when you can accomplish many of the goals your group may have set. The only fly in the ointment may be a certain resistance to change, especially when it is suggested by a newcomer.

Eventually, all committed groups face the stage of Transformation. Anundsen and Shaffer suggest that groups can change in any of three ways: They may segment, expand, or disband. Many salons end up segmenting, perhaps forming secondary groups to concentrate on writing, creative play, or new methods of interacting. Other salons expand, either because members long for greater diversity or because they want to connect with society at large. The urge to become more actively involved in politics or social issues is a form of expansion.

Whether it's in five months or fifty years, every salon will come to an end. If a group disbands because it failed to meet members' expectations, it probably never quite jelled as a community. Salonist Helen White summed up the prevailing attitude at one salon that dissolved after a short time:

> I suspect we had a problem that may be more acute in university-laden areas like ours. Many of us have plenty of folks to discuss issues with in our everyday lives; we were drawn to the salon idea more because of the community-building aspect. And when community didn't envelop us after three or four months—well, the whole thing was taking too long! Where was the payoff? So, many of us dropped out to take a running leap at some other activity that may provide that elusive sense of belonging— and fast!

Even salons that have expended the time and effort to achieve genuine community end eventually. They end when the people in them grow older, move away, or die. They end when they cease to serve a purpose in people's lives. They often end at times of cataclysmic social change—in wartime, for instance—when relationships and identities are up for grabs.

Not to worry, though. Your salon can extend its lifetime by remaining open to new members, new ideas, and new identities for itself—and by providing a relaxed, realistic, humane environment. Perhaps the healthiest attitude is keen interest in what's happening right now, without fretting unduly about the future.

SALONS IN SOCIETY: MAKING A DIFFERENCE

It's a mistake to think of salons as action groups, but it's not a mistake to think that action can arise from salons.

~ Erika Sukstorf, guerrilla salonist

Salons and salonists have repeatedly demonstrated the capacity to move from talk to action. Following the April 1992 riots in Los Angeles, many salonists there were "shocked into the awareness that our community was going up in flames," as salonist Ronny Barkay put it. Salon members began to discuss what community really meant to them, and many became interested in actively responding to the needs of the city. Individuals from various groups in the region formed the Creative Action Salon, which directed its efforts toward getting people to vote and establishing a time-dollar bartering co-op. The members also sent an open letter to the media, suggesting the formation of a citizens broadcasting commission to pay attention to media portrayals of the community.

Barkay and Erika Sukstorf then contacted community members through computer bulletin boards and founded the Next Step, a multicultural, nonprofit organization seeking permanent self-help solutions to long-standing problems in the inner city. Several salon members joined the Next Step, contributing their expertise in writing, public relations, and fund-raising to set up a program that helped businesses affected by the riots obtain loans. They also conducted classes for teenagers and businesspeople in financial survival, computer use, and other means to empowerment.

Conversational groups that are formed in order to discuss specific social or political issues often take action more quickly than salons that meet for more general conversation. The study circle model in particular has been effective around the world—particularly when the circles have focused on citizenship, human rights, health education, or literacy. From 1930 through the late 1960s, the Metis, an indigenous people in Canada, created their own materials for study circles, discussing and proposing solutions to the economic and social problems that beset them, including their treaty relationship with the Canadian government. The circles also did much to rekindle in the Metis an appreciation of their history and values as a people.

Citizenship School, developed by Esau Jenkins and Bernice Robinson in South Carolina, focused on literacy for African Americans. The school's study of fundamental documents of government, such as the Declaration of Independence and the United Nations Declaration of Human Rights, sparked extraordinary discussions of what citizenship means. By organizing small community study groups, participants learned an array of skills that they later put to use in forming civil rights groups. The communities involved experienced a "dramatic decline in the levels of crime and social pathology," according to a subsequent study.

Swedish study circle organizations have supported successful programs beyond the country's borders. In Tanzania, for example, Swedes trained discussion leaders, provided study materials, and gave administrative support to circles that encouraged Tanzanian citizens to read, debate, and vote. Between the late 1960s and 1981, the literacy rate in Tanzania rose from 20 percent to 80 percent—thanks in part to these study circles. In addition, a health and sanitation campaign initiated in the early 1970s trained 75,000 study circle leaders over an eighteen-month period. Radio programs and printed booklets were then used as the bases for study. An estimated 2 million people took part in weekly discussions throughout the country.

The National Issues Forums have produced issue-oriented books to be used in salon-style adult literacy classes in American correctional institutions. Reading about and discussing "The Drug Crisis," "Growing Up at Risk," and AIDS has helped the volunteer inmates develop their speaking skills, their sense of self-worth, and a feeling of participating in a wider community. Cohousing groups in Denmark and the United States have built small, cooperative communities whose viability is maintained through conversation.

STEPS TOWARD ACTIVISM

Salon activism may begin after a group has been together for several years and the members have come to trust each other. The salonists may arrange to work together on small, coordinated projects, such as letter-writing campaigns or volunteer work at a shelter for the homeless. Jim and Nicole Fary, members of a Maryland salon, reported that their salon participated in Montgomery County's annual volunteer day by preparing food packages for homeless people. An Arlington, Virginia, salon painted the stairwell for a day-care center, cohosted a picnic for homeless children, and marched in a prochoice demonstration in Washington, D.C. Too small? Not at all. Social change is often triggered by incremental actions like these, which gather momentum and eventually become a movement. The smallest project your salon undertakes could have unforeseen and significant consequences.

Salonists may be sparked to action, as were Barkay and Sukstorf, by an event or issue: a natural disaster, a civil disturbance, new laws or political candidates coming up for a vote. Even if the entire salon does not commit to action, concerned members may form a politically active subgroup. No matter how passionate they feel about large issues, such groups in most cases ought to limit themselves to short-term, specific, and focused efforts, grounding all their actions in consensus. To enhance their influence, subgroups might consider joining forces with established, financially stable nonprofit organizations that tackle the same issue. Salonists generally find that their interpersonal and organizing skills are highly valued by grassroots networks and other activist groups.

It's best to be cautious about tackling projects that do not have the support of the whole group or that seem too challenging for the group's resources. Without shared history, a durable sense of community, and the solidarity of consensus, groups that begin as conversational gatherings may be unable to withstand the pres-

> Social change is often triggered by incremental actions, which gather momentum and eventually become a movement. The smallest project your salon undertakes could have unforeseen and significant consequences.

sures of political involvement. Taking concerted action on a regional basis is even more difficult. Rarely are all members of all salons in a region ready to take the same action at the same time. Many salonists feel highly protective of the distinctive role of their salon, and rightly so. If your salon prefers to stick with the entirely legitimate function of providing a haven for egalitarian conversation, don't apologize—you're furthering your values in an equally important way.

Indeed, some salons form specifically as an antidote to activist burnout—to discuss issues other than those in which they are directly involved, to form friendships, and to return to the tasks of building a better world with renewed vigor. Salonist Mary Ruthsdotter has been a member of one such group. "Another action-oriented group wasn't what we were after," she explained. "And one ground rule was quickly articulated: Our discussions would not leave us frustrated, stymied, negative, or depressed about the world!"

If your salon is contemplating action on an issue, perhaps the best advice, aside from starting small and advancing by small steps, is to take the time to assess the effect of your efforts on the salon itself. If the action is becoming a threat to solidarity and community, changes will be needed. The point is to keep all of your salon values in balance.

SALONS AND CITIZENSHIP

In the past century, the most important issue that has faced humankind has been figuring out the mechanisms of production. In the next hundred years, it will be the mechanisms of cooperation.

~ Adam Jacobs, salonist

Imagine a world in which salons meet regularly in every inhabited square mile. Imagine people visiting salons as frequently as they buy or gather food. Imagine all of us talking, searching for solutions to social problems, and enjoying the support of colleagues and friends when we attempt to realize our ideas. Imagine governments turning to salonists for counsel on decisions that affect community life. Imagine everyone voting. Imagine sharing tools, meals, and cars up and down the block. Imagine a society in which no one fears criticism when they open their mouths to sing, lift their skirts to dance, set their pens to paper, or stand before a crowd to speak.

We're not there yet, but there are encouraging signs. In 1997 and 1998, for example, forty-five study circles throughout Miami addressed the hot-button issue of immigration and its effect on one of America's most turbulently multicultural cities. With help from the Topsfield Foundation's Congressional Exchange Program, which brings discussion salons together with elected representatives, Miami study circle leaders and members met with U.S. Representative Lincoln Diaz-Balart—not in a typical screaming-match public meeting, but in a jumbo salon that began with a "fishbowl" (see chapter 9) with Diaz-Balart and the study circle leaders, then expanded out to include all the members in attendance. Participants talked, with civility and candor instead of anger, about crimes against immigrants, the impact of multiculturalism on Miami's schools, job competition between immigrants and the native-born, and the effect of the immigrant influx on already-existing racial and ethnic tensions in the Dade County metropolis. "This approach is much more productive," said Diaz-Balart, "and I hope more of it goes on." Later, study circles were formed in seventeen area high schools to look into the same issues, and teachers have been considering making this form of saloning a regular part of the curriculum.

A long way from the days when perfumed, powdered, and peruked members of the French beau monde gathered to talk—and yet not so long a way. Whatever their composition, the best salons have been seismographs of social change, sensitive instruments for recording, and often furthering, the earthshaking alterations in politics, consciousness, and desire that make human history. It is all still happening today—and it's just a living room away.

SALON NETWORKS: A CHALLENGE

As salons became increasingly widespread in the mid-1990s, spurred in large part by *Utne Reader* and its Neighborhood Salon Association, which provided salonists in a given area with names and addresses of others interested in organized conversation, regional networks were created. They've operated in parts of Northern and Southern California, Washington, Virginia, New York, New Jersey, and Washington, D.C. Some have included up to forty salons in some degree of regular contact with one another. Salonists visited other groups; two or three salons would get together for joint weekend retreats. Facilitators met to swap tips on salon leadership.

Sad to say, all the regional salon networks are dead today, victims of lack of time, lack of interest, rebellions against overcontrolling organizers—many of the problems, in short, that bring salons themselves to closure. While salonists can still obtain copies of "The Salon-keeper's Companion" from the magazine, the NSA is no more and *Utne's* salon efforts have metamorphosed into a very large and active online community, Café Utne (www.utne.com/cafe). Some salonists use Café Utne to keep in touch with one another, but there is at this writing no up-to-date central database of salons nation- or even region-wide. This is one of the biggest challenges the salon movement faces today, a challenge that's waiting for an ambitious and dedicated individual, group, or organization to take it on.

APPENDIX

RESOURCES

Books, organizations, and other resources for building and maintaining salons. For books, full information is provided in the bibliography.

THE HISTORY OF SALONS

Janine Bouissounouse, *Julie; The Life of Mademoiselle de Lespinasse: Her Salon, Her Friends, Her Loves,* translated by Pierre de Fontnouvelle

Margaret Case Harriman, *The Vicious Circle*

J. Christopher Herold, *Mistress to an Age: A Life of Madame de Staël*

Amelia Ruth Gere Mason, *The Women of the French Salons*

Peter Quennell, ed., *Affairs of the Mind: The Salon in Europe and America from the Eighteenth to the Twentieth Century*

SALON-RELATED FICTION AND MEMOIRS

Natalie Clifford Barney, *Pensées d'une Amazon* ("Thoughts of an Amazon")
A memoir.

Sylvia Beach, *Shakespeare and Company*
A memoir.

Lord Byron, *The Blues: A Literary Eclogue*
A comedy satirizing the British bluestockings and their salons.

Ramón de la Cruz, *Sainete: Las Tertulias de Madrid*
A late-eighteenth-century play satirizing the Spanish salons known as *tertulias.*

Max Eastman, *Venture*
Includes a description of Mabel Dodge's salon.

Ramón Gómez de la Serna, *Pombo*
Recollections of the tertulia at Café Pombo, written in 1918.

Benito Pérez Galdós, *La Estafeta Romántica*
An 1899 novel including references to tertulias.

Benito Pérez Galdós, *The Golden Fountain Cafe (La Fontana de Oro)*
An 1890 novel with a humorous description of a revolutionary tertulia.

Langston Hughes, *The Big Sea*
>An autobiography including descriptions of the personalities and gatherings of the Harlem Renaissance.

Aldous Huxley, *Crome Yellow*
>Includes a caricature of the salon hosted by Ottoline Morrell.

D.H. Lawrence, *The Plumed Serpent*
>Includes a character based on Mabel Dodge.

D.H. Lawrence, *Women in Love*
>Includes a caricature of Lady Ottoline Morrell.

Marty Martin, *Gertrude Stein Gertrude Stein Gertrude Stein: A One-Character Play*
>A play based on Gertrude Stein's autobiographical writings.

Ramón de Mesonero Romanos, *Memorias de un Setentón*
>An 1880 autobiography including an account of tertulias in the 1830s.

Molière, *The Learned Ladies* (*Les Précieuses Ridicules*)
>A play satirizing salon society.

Marcel Proust, *Remembrance of Things Past*
>A magisterial novel of society and salons.

Michel de Pure, *La Prètieuse*
>A novel based on poet Madame de la Suze's salon.

Gertrude Stein, *The Autobiography of Alice B. Toklas*
>Includes descriptions of the Stein salon/studio in Paris.

Wallace Thurman, *Infants of the Spring*
>A novel set in the milieu of the Harlem Renaissance.

Carl Van Vechten, *Nigger Heaven*
>A novel about the Harlem Renaissance period, featuring Alelia Walker as the character Adora Boniface.

INCREASING GROUP DIVERSITY AND UNDERSTANDING

BOOKS

Clyde W. Ford, *We Can All Get Along: Fifty Steps You Can Take to Help End Racism*
>A list of ideas useful for a group that wants to expand membership diversity and/or increase members' understanding of racism.

Rick Simonson and Scott Walker, eds., *The Graywolf Annual Five: Multicultural Literacy: Opening the American Mind*
>Essays on diversity and racism accompanied by an excellent list of what everyone should know about cultures around the world.

ORGANIZATIONS

Center for Conflict Resolution
> 731 State Street, Madison, WI 53703
> Provides resources for nonviolent conflict resolution and consensus decision making.

Foundation for Community Encouragement, Inc.
> Box 50518, Knoxville, TN 37950-0518
> 615/690-4334
> www.fce-community.org
> Founded by author and therapist M. Scott Peck.

National Council for International Visitors
> 1420 K Street NW, Suite 800, Washington DC 20005-2401
> 800/523-8101
> www.usia.gov/usiahome/usia-state/nciv.html
> Guides for contacting international visitors in your state.

Tools for Change
> 349 Church St., San Francisco, CA 94114
> 415/861-6387
> www.toolsforchange.org
> Provides training and resources for groups and organizations.

COMMUNICATIONS AND GROUP DYNAMICS

BOOKS

Sedonia Cahill and Joshua Halpern, *The Ceremonial Circle: Practice, Ritual, and Renewal for Personal and Community Healing*

Sam Kaner et al., *Facilitator's Guide to Participatory Decision-Making*

Joanna R. Macy and Molly Young Brown, *Coming Back to Life: Practices to Reconnect Our Lives, Our World*

M. Scott Peck, *The Different Drum: Community-Making and Peace*

Michael J. Sheeran, *Beyond Majority Rule*
> An excellent book on the ins and outs of the Quaker methods of decision making and interacting at meetings.

ORGANIZATIONS

The Ojai Foundation
> Box 1620, Ojai, CA 93023
> Booklets and workshops on using council methods.

STUDY CIRCLES

ORGANIZATIONS

Chautauqua Institution
>   Box 28, One Ames Ave., Chautauqua, NY 14722
>   www.chautauqua-inst.org
>   Historical information on Chautauquas; a host of summer education and entertainment programs.

Elderhostel
>   75 Federal Street, Boston, MA 02110-1941
>   www.elderhostel.org
>   Educational programs in many locations, primarily for senior citizens.

National Issues Forums
>   100 Commons Road, Dayton, OH 45459-2777
>   800/433-7834
>   www.nifi.org
>   Organization devoted to making study circles accessible and widespread. Provides English and Spanish language study materials, and conveys opinions of study circle participants to policy makers.

Study Circles Resource Center
>   Box 203, Route 169, Pomfret, CT 06258
>   860/928-2616
>   civic.net/ACF/SCRC.html
>   Materials, support, and technical assistance, primarily for community-wide study circle programs. Their booklet, *Guidelines for Organizing and Leading a Study Circle,* is particularly useful.

The Union Institute Office of Social Responsibility
>   Center for Public Policy
>   1731 Connecticut Ave. NW, Washington, DC 20009-1146
>   202/667-1313
>   www.tui.edu/OSR/index.html

Watson Institute
>   Brown University
>   Box 1948, Providence, RI 02912
>   401/863-3465
>   www.brown.edu/Departments/Watson_Institute
>   Research and information on foreign policy.

CREATIVITY AND PLAY

BOOKS

Thomas Armstrong, *Seven Kinds of Smart: Identifying and Developing Your Many Intelligences*
Includes lists of games and exercises that could easily be adapted to creativity salons.

Alastair Brotchie, comp., and Mel Gooding, ed., *Surrealist Games*
This wonderful box of word and drawing games invented by the surrealists is available at many museum gift shops and some book and game stores.

James Charlton, *Charades: The Complete Guide to America's Favorite Party Game*
Complete, easy to follow, and humorously written.

Exploratorium Teacher Institute, *The Exploratorium Science Snackbook*
A great sourcebook for creative science play.

Stephen Nachmanovitch, *Free Play: Improvisation in Life and Art*
Inspiring essays on creativity and play, together with a few exercises.

Milton E. Polsky, *Let's Improvise: Becoming Creative, Expressive, and Spontaneous Through Drama*
Theater exercises.

Jo Miles Schuman, *Art from Many Hands: Multicultural Art Projects*
An excellent book explaining a wide range of unusual and beautiful art and craft projects from around the world.

Viola Spolin, *Improvisation for the Theater: A Handbook of Teaching and Directing Techniques*
Written for professional acting teachers. Filled with exercises and theater games that could easily be adapted for use in a salon.

Barbara Steinwachs and Sivasailam Thiagarajan, *Barnga: A Simulation Game on Cultural Clashes*
Available through the Intercultural Press, Box 700, Yarmouth, ME 04096.

BOOK CLUBS

BOOKS

A Great Books Primer: Essays on Liberal Education, the Uses of Discussion, and Rules for Reading
Available from the Great Books Foundation, 35 East Wacker Drive, Suite 2300, Chicago, IL 60601-2298 800/222-5870.

Rachel W. Jacobsohn, *The Reading Group Handbook: Everything You Need to Know to Start Your Own Book Club*

Rollene Saal, *The New York Public Library Guide to Reading Groups*
Nuts and bolts, carefully presented.

Ellen Slezak, ed., *The Book Group Book*
Illuminating stories of real book groups and how they work.

ONLINE COMMUNITIES

BOOKS

Cliff Figallo, *Hosting Web Communities*
First-rate advice from a cybersalonist who's seen it all.

Stacy Horn, *Cyberville: Clicks, Culture, and the Creation of an Online Town*
Sharp, even racy, tales of the creation of the Echo online community in New York.

Steven Johnson, *Interface Culture: How New Technology Transforms the Way We Create and Communicate*

Amy Joe Kim, *Community Building on the Web*

Howard Rheingold, *The Virtual Community: Homesteading on the Electronic Frontier*
An early work, still readable for its generous vision of online community.

SITES

Café Utne
www.cafe.utne.com/cafe/
E-salons and other online activities.

CIX
www1.cix.co.uk/
Long-lived British Web community.

Echo
www.echonyc.com
New York's premier community.

ForumOne
forumone.com
Premier search engine for online communities. A one-stop shopping center for finding Web-talk opportunities.

MetaNetwork
www.tmn.com
Virginia-based community.

The WELL (Whole Earth 'Lectronic Link)
www.well.com
Pioneering, now legendary, California-based community.

BIBLIOGRAPHY

Abrahams, Roger D. *The Man-of-Words in the West Indies: Performance and the Emergence of Creole Culture*. Baltimore: The Johns Hopkins University Press, 1983.

Adair, Margo. *Meditations on Everything Under the Sun: The Dance of Imagination, Intuition, and Mindfulness*. Gabriola Island, BC: New Society Publishers, 2001.

Adair, Margo. *Working Inside Out: Tools for Change*. Berkeley, Calif.: Wingbow Press, 1984.

Adair, Margo, and Sharon Howell. *The Subjective Side of Politics*. Pamphlet, no date. San Francisco: Tools for Change.

Aldis, Janet. *Madame Geoffrin: Her Salon and Her Times, 1750–1777*. New York: Putnam; London: Methuen & Co., 1905.

Alexander, Christopher, et al. *A Pattern Language: Towns, Buildings, Construction*. New York: Oxford University Press, 1977.

Altmann, Alexander. *Moses Mendelssohn: A Biographical Study*. 1973. Portland, Oreg.: Littman Library of Jewish Civilization, 1998.

Anderson, Margaret C. *My Thirty Years' War*. 1930. Westport, Conn.: Greenwood, 1971.

——. *The Strange Necessity: The Autobiography, Resolutions and Reminiscence to 1969*. New York: Horizon Press, 1970.

Apple, Michael W. *Official Knowledge: Democratic Education in a Conservative Age*. New York: Routledge, 1993.

Apte, Mahadev L. *Humor and Laughter: An Anthropological Approach*. Ithaca, N.Y.: Cornell University Press, 1985.

Arendt, Hannah. *Rahel Varnhagen: The Life of a Jewess*. Trans. Richard and Clara Winston. 1958. Baltimore: The Johns Hopkins University Press, 1997.

Ariès, Philippe, and Georges Duby, eds. *A History of Private Life*, Vols. I–V. Cambridge, Mass.: The Belknap Press of Harvard University Press, 1987–1991.

Armstrong, Thomas. *Seven Kinds of Smart: Identifying and Developing Your Many Intelligences*. Revised and updated, New York: Plume, 1999.

Aronson, Nicole. *Mademoiselle de Scudéry*. Trans. Stuart R. Aronson. Boston: Twayne, 1978.

Barker, Robert G. *Ecological Psychology: Concepts and Methods for Studying the Environment of Human Behavior.* Stanford, Calif.: Stanford University Press, 1968.

Barney, Natalie Clifford. *Pensées d'une Amazone.* Paris: Émile-Paul, 1920.

Barreca, Regina. *They Used to Call Me Snow White—But I Drifted: Women's Strategic Use of Humor.* New York: Viking, 1991.

Bauman, Richard, and Joel Sherzer, eds. *Explorations in the Ethnography of Speaking.* Second edition, New York: Cambridge University Press, 1989.

Beach, Sylvia. *Shakespeare and Company.* 1959. Lincoln: University of Nebraska Press, 1991.

Beck, Peggy V., and A.L. Walters. *The Sacred: Ways of Knowledge, Sources of Life.* Tsaile, Ariz.: Navajo Community College, 1977.

Bellah, Robert N., et al. *Habits of the Heart: Individualism and Commitment in American Life.* Updated with a new introduction. Berkeley: University of California Press, 1996.

Berendt, John. "The Salon." *Esquire,* November 1990.

Bianco, Frank. *Voices of Silence: Lives of the Trappists Today.* New York: Paragon House, 1991; Anchor Books, 1992.

Blennerhassett, Charlotte Julia von Leyden, Lady. *Madame de Staël: Her Friends and Her Influence in Politics and Literature,* 3 vols. London: Chapman and Hall Ltd., 1889.

Bloch, Maurice, ed. *Political Language and Oratory in Traditional Society.* New York: Academic Press, 1975.

Bohm, David. "On Dialogue." *Noetic Science Review,* Autumn 1992.

Bohm, David, and Mark Edwards. *Changing Consciousness: Exploring the Hidden Source of the Social, Political and Environmental Crises Facing our World.* San Francisco: HarperSanFranciso, 1991.

Bohm, David, and F. David Peat. *Science, Order, and Creativity.* New York: Bantam Books, 1987.

Bostick, Alan. "Word of Mouth." *The Tennessean,* May 16, 1993.

Bouissounouse, Janine. *Julie; The Life of Mademoiselle de Lespinasse: Her Salon, Her Friends, Her Loves.* Trans. Pierre de Fontnouvelle. New York: Appleton-Century-Crofts, 1962.

Bradbrook, M.C. *The School of Night: A Study in the Literary Relationships of Sir Walter Raleigh.* New York: Russell & Russell, 1965.

Breggin, Peter R. *Beyond Conflict: From Self-Help and Psychotherapy to Peacemaking.* New York: St. Martin's, 1992.

Brotchie, Alastair, comp., and Mel Gooding, ed. *A Book of Surrealist Games: Including the Little Surrealist Dictionary.* Boston: Shambhala Redstone, 1995.

Brown, Dorothy M. *Setting a Course: American Women in the 1920s*. Boston: Twayne, 1987.

Byron, George Gordon, Lord. "The Blues: A Literary Eclogue," in *The Works of Lord Byron*. Ed. Ernest Hartley Coleridge. Vol. 4. London: John Murray, 1901.

Cahill, Sedonia, and Joshua Halpern. *The Ceremonial Circle: Practice, Ritual, and Renewal for Personal and Community Healing*. San Francisco: HarperSanFrancisco, 1992.

Campbell, Paul Newell. *Rhetoric — Ritual: A Study of the Communicative and Aesthetic Dimensions of Language*. Belmont, Calif.: Dickenson, 1972.

Carbaugh, Donal, ed. *Cultural Communication and Intercultural Contact*. Hillsdale, N.J.: L. Erlbaum, 1990.

Carr, Phillip. *Days with the French Romantics in the Paris of 1830*. London: Methuen, 1932.

Charlton, James. *Charades: The Complete Guide to America's Favorite Party Game*. New York: Harper and Row, 1983.

Craveri, Benedetta. "Conqueror of Paris." *The New York Review of Books*, December 17, 1992.

Crocker, Lester G. *Diderot: The Embattled Philosopher*. 1954. New York: Free Press, 1966.

Crunden, Robert M. *American Salons: Encounters with European Modernism, 1885–1917*. New York: Oxford University Press, 1993.

Cruz, Ramón de la. *Sainete: Las Tertulias de Madrid*. Madrid: Taurus, 1985.

Csikszentmihalyi, Mihaly. *Flow: The Psychology of Optimal Experience*. New York: Harper & Row, 1990.

Curiel, Roberta, and Bernard Dov Cooperman. *The Venetian Ghetto*. New York: Rizzoli, 1990.

De Bono, Edward. *Future Positive*. London: M. Temple Smith, 1979.

——. *Practical Thinking: Four Ways to be Right, Five Ways to be Wrong, Five Ways to Understand*. New York: Penguin, 1971.

De Maré, Patrick B., et al. *Koinonia: From Hate, through Dialogue, to Culture in the Large Group*. New York: Karnac, 1991.

Diaz, Adriana. *Freeing the Creative Spirit: Drawing on the Power of Art to Tap the Magic and Wisdom Within*. San Francisco: HarperSanFrancisco, 1992.

Drennan, Robert E., ed. *The Algonquin Wits*. New York: Citadel Press, 1968.

Duncan, Hugh Dalziel. *Communication and Social Order*. 1970. With a new introduction by Carol Wilder. New Brunswick: Tranaction, 1985.

Eastman, Max. *Enjoyment of Living*. New York: Harper, 1948.

——. *Venture*. New York: Boni, 1927.

Eisler, Benita. *O'Keeffe and Stieglitz: An American Romance.* New York: Doubleday, 1991.

Emigh, Phyliss. "Kindred Souls or Kissing Cousins?: SCRC's Interpretation of Study Circles Does Not Always Match the Swedish Model." *FOCUS on Study Circles: The Newsletter of the SCRC,* Winter 1991.

Epstein, Seymour. *You're Smarter than You Think: How to Develop Your Practical Intelligence for Success in Living.* New York: Simon & Schuster, 1993.

Estes, Caroline. "Consensus Ingredients." *In Context,* Fall 1983.

Exploratorium Teacher Institute. *The Exploratorium Science Snackbook.* San Francisco: Exploratorium, 1991.

Farb, Peter. *Word Play: What Happens When People Talk.* New York: Vintage, 1993.

Feldman, Reynold, and Cynthia Voelke, comps. and eds. *A World Treasury of Folk Wisdom.* San Francisco: HarperSanFrancisco, 1992.

Fielding, Daphne. *Those Remarkable Cunards: Emerald and Nancy.* New York: Atheneum, 1968.

Figallo, Cliff. *Hosting Web Communities: Building Relationships, Increasing Customer Loyalty, and Maintaining a Competitive Edge.* New York: John Wiley and Sons, 1998.

Fitch, Noel Riley. *Sylvia Beach and the Lost Generation: A History of Literary Paris in the Twenties and Thirties.* New York: Norton, 1983.

Ford, Clyde W. *We Can All Get Along: Fifty Steps You Can Take to Help End Racism.* New York: Dell, 1994.

Furbank, P.N. *Diderot: A Critical Biography.* New York: Knopf, 1992.

Gang, Philip S., et al. *Conscious Education: The Bridge to Freedom.* Grafton, Vt.: Dagaz, 1992.

Garfield, Charles A., et al. *Wisdom Circles: A Guide to Self-Discovery and Community Building in Small Groups.* New York: Hyperion, 1998.

Garvey, Timothy J. *Public Sculptor: Lorado Taft and the Beautification of Chicago.* Urbana: University of Illinois Press, 1988.

Gatto, John Taylor. *Dumbing Us Down: The Hidden Curriculum of Compulsory Schooling.* Philadelphia: New Society, 1992.

Gerard, Glenna, and Linda Ellinor. *Dialogue: Rediscover the Transforming Power of Conversation.* New York: John Wiley and Sons, 1998.

Gómez de la Serna, Ramón. *Greguerías: The Wit and Wisdom of Ramón Gómez de la Serna.* Edited by Philip Ward. New York: Oleander Press, 1982.

———. *Pombo: Biografía del Célebre Café y de Otros Cafés Famosos.* Barcelona: Editorial Juventud, 1960.

Grauman, Brigid. "The Mobile Guide: The Thinking Person's Hotel." *Wall Street Journal*, February 5, 1993.

Great Books Foundation. *A Great Books Primer: Essays on Liberal Education, the Uses of Discussion, and Rules for Reading.* Chicago: Great Books Foundation, 1955.

Grillo, Paul Jacques. *Form, Function, and Design.* New York: Dover, 1975.

Gross, Ron. "Salons Belong in Libraries." *Adult and Continuing Education Today*, August 26, 1991.

Hall, Edward T. *Beyond Culture.* New York: Anchor, 1989.

Hall, Mildred Reed, and Edward T. Hall. *The Fourth Dimension in Architecture: The Impact of Building on Behavior.* Santa Fe, N.Mex.: Sunstone, 1995.

Hapgood, Hutchins. *A Victorian in the Modern World.* 1939. Republished with a new introduction by Robert Allen Skotheim. Seattle: University of Washington Press, 1972.

Hargrave, Mary. *Some German Women and Their Salons.* London: T.W. Laurie, 1912.

Harkins, William E. *Karel Capek.* New York: Columbia University Press, 1962.

Harriman, Margaret Case. *The Vicious Circle: The Story of the Algonquin Round Table.* New York: Rinehart, 1951.

Hart, John E. *Floyd Dell.* New York: Twayne, 1971.

Heath, Lillian M, comp. *Eighty Pleasant Evenings.* Boston: United Society of Christian Endeavor, 1898.

Hedges, Elaine. *Hearts and Hands: Women, Quilts, and American Society. Based on the film by Pat Ferrero.* Nashville, Tenn.: Rutledge, 1996.

Heider, John. *The Tao of Leadership: Lao Tzu's Tao Te Ching Adapted for a New Age.* Atlanta: Humanics New Age, 1985.

Herold, J. Christopher. *Mistress to an Age: A Life of Madame de Staël.* 1958. Revised, with an introduction by Rebecca West. Alexandria, Va.: Time-Life, 1981.

Hillman, James, and Michael Ventura. *We've Had a Hundred Years of Psychotherapy—and the World's Getting Worse.* San Francisco: HarperSanFranciso, 1992.

Hipp, Earl. *The Caring Circle: A Facilitator's Guide to Support Groups, Based on the Book* Feed Your Head. Center City, Minn.: Hazelden, 1992.

Hofmann, Paul. *The Viennese: Splendor, Twilight, and Exile.* New York: Anchor, 1989.

Hope, Anne, and Sally Timmel. *Training for Transformation: A Handbook for Community Workers.* 1984. Zimbabwe: Intermediate Technology, 1999.

Horn, Stacy. *Cyberville: Clicks, Culture, and the Creation of an Online Town.* New York: Warner, 1998.

Howard, Alice, and Walden Howard. *Exploring the Road Less Traveled: A Study Guide for Small Groups, a Workbook for Individuals, a Step-by-Step Guide for Group Leaders.* Forward by M. Scott Peck. New York: Simon & Schuster, 1985.

Hudson, William J. *Intellectual Capital: How to Build It, Enhance It, Use It.* New York: John Wiley and Sons, 1993.

Hughes, Langston. *The Big Sea, an Autobiography.* 1963. New York: Hill and Wang, 1993.

Huxley, Aldous. *Crome Yellow and Other Works.* New York: Harper and Row, 1983.

Ilardo, Joseph W. *Risk-Taking for Personal Growth: A Step-by-Step Workbook.* Oakland, Calif.: New Harbinger, 1992.

Jacobsohn, Rachel W. *The Reading Group Handbook: Everything You Need to Know to Start Your Own Book Club.* New York: Hyperion, 1998.

Jay, Karla. *The Amazon and the Page: Natalie Clifford Barney and Renée Vivien.* Bloomington: Indiana University Press, 1988.

Johnson, Steven. *Interface Culture: How New Technology Transforms the Way We Create and Communicate.* San Franciso: HarperEdge, 1997.

Johnston, Charles M. *Necessary Wisdom: Meeting the Challenge of a New Cultural Maturity.* Seattle: ICD; Berkeley, Calif.: Celestial Arts, 1991.

Kalweit, Holger. *Shamans, Healers, and Medicine Men.* Translated by Michael H. Kohn. Boston: Shambhala, 1992.

Kaner, Sam, with Lenny Lind, Duane Berger, Catherine Toldi & Sarah Fisk, *Facilitator's Guide to Participatory Decision-Making.* Gabriola Island, BC: New Society Publishers, 1996.

Karpeles, Gustav. *Jewish Literature, and Other Essays.* 1895. Freeport, N.Y.: Books for Libraries, 1971.

Keating, L. Clark. *Studies on the Literary Salon in France, 1550–1615.* Cambridge, Mass.: Harvard University Press, 1941.

Kessler, Shelley. "The Mysteries Program: Educating Adolescents for Today's World." *Holistic Education Review,* Winter 1990.

Kim, Amy Joe. *Community Building on the Web: Secret Strategies for Successful Online Communities.* Berkeley, Calif.: Peachpit Press, 1999.

Lakoff, George, and Mark Johnson. *Metaphors We Live By.* Chicago: University of Chicago Press, 1980.

Laskin, David, and Holly Hughes. *The Reading Group Book: The Complete Guide to Starting and Sustaining a Reading Group.* New York: Plume, 1995.

Lawrence, D.H. *Quetzalcoatl*. Originally published in 1926 as *The Plumed Serpent*. Ed. with an introduction by Louis L. Martz. New York: New Directions, 1998.

———. *Women in Love*. 1920. New York: Doubleday; Modern Library, 1999.

Levaillant, Maurice. *The Passionate Exiles: Madame de Staël and Madame Récamier*. Trans. Malcolm Barnes. 1958. Freeport, N.Y.: Books for Libraries, 1971.

Leviton, Richard. "Reconcilable Differences." *Yoga Journal*, Sept./Oct. 1992.

Lougee, Carolyn C. *Le Paradis des Femmes: Women, Salons, and Social Stratification in Seventeenth-Century France*. Princeton, N.J.: Princeton University Press, 1976.

Luhan, Mabel Dodge. *A History of Having a Great Many Times Not Continued to Be Friends: The Correspondence Between Mable Dodge and Gertrude Stein, 1911–1934*. Ed. Patricia R. Everett. Albuquerque: University of New Mexico Press, 1996.

———. *Intimate Memories: The Autobiography of Mable Dodge*. 1933–1937. Ed. Lois Palkin Rudnick. Albuquerque: University of New Mexico Press, 1999.

Lund, Jens, and Elizabeth Simpson, eds. *Folk Arts of Washington State: A Survey of Contemporary Folk Arts and Artists in the State of Washington*. Tumwater: Washington State Folklife Council, 1989.

Luvmour, Sambhava, and Josette Luvmour. *Everyone Wins!: Cooperative Games and Activities*. Philadelphia: New Society, 1990.

Macy, Joanna. *Widening Circles: A Memoir*. Gabriola Island, BC: New Society Publishers, 2000.

Macy, Joanna R. and Molly Young Brown. *Coming Back to Life: Practices to Reconnect Our Lives, Our World*. Gabriola Island, BC: New Society Publishers, 1998.

Marchese, John. "From Muffin Shop to Salon." *New York Times*, May 30, 1993.

Martin, Marty. *Gertrude Stein Gertrude Stein Gertrude Stein: A One-Character Play*. New York: Vintage, 1980.

Mason, Amelia Ruth Gere. *The Women of the French Salons*. New York: The Century Co., 1891.

May, Henry F. *The End of American Innocence: A Study of the First Years of Our Own Time, 1912–1917*. 1959. New York: Columbia University Press, 1992.

Mesonero Romanos, Ramón de. *Memorias de un Setentón*. 1880. Madrid: Editorial Castalia: Comunidad de Madrid, 1994.

Mills, Eugene S. *The Story of Elderhostel*. Hanover, N.H.: University Press of New England, 1993.

Mills, Stephanie. "Salons and Their Keepers." *CoEvolution Quarterly*, Summer 1974.

Mindell, Arnold. *The Leader as Martial Artist: An Introduction to Deep Democracy*. San Francisco: HarperSanFrancisco, 1992.

Modena, Leone. *The Autobiography of a Seventeenth-Century Venetian Rabbi: Leon Modena's Life of Judah*. Translated and edited by Mark R. Cohen. Princeton, N.J.: Princeton University Press, 1988.

Molière. *The Learned Ladies (Les Précieuses Ridicules)*. Trans. A.R. Waller. London: Nick Hern, 1996.

Morrell, Ottoline. *Ottoline at Garsington: Memoirs of Lady Ottoline Morrell, 1915–1918*. Ed. Robert Gathorne-Hardy. New York: Knopf, 1975.

Myers, Sylvia Harcstark. *The Bluestocking Circle: Women, Friendship, and the Life of the Mind in Eighteenth-Century England*. Oxford: Clarendon Press; New York: Oxford University Press, 1990.

Nachmanovitch, Stephen. *Free Play: Improvisation in Life and Art*. Los Angeles: Tarcher, 1990.

Natanson, Maurice Alexander, ed. *Philosophy, Rhetoric and Argumentation*. University Park: Pennsylvania State University Press, 1965.

Oldenburg, Ray. *The Great Good Place: Cafés, Coffee Shops, Bookstores, Bars, Hair Salons, and Other Hangouts at the Heart of a Community*. New York: Marlow, 1999.

Oliver, Leonard P. *Study Circles: Coming Together for Personal Growth and Social Change*. Cabin John, Md.: Seven Locks Press, 1987.

Pearlman, Mickey. *What to Read: The Essential Guide for Reading Group Members and Other Book Lovers*. Rev. edition. New York: HarperPerennial, 1999.

Peck, M. Scott. *The Different Drum: Community-Making and Peace*. New York: Simon & Schuster, 1987.

Pérez Galdós, Benito. *La Estafeta Romántica*. In *Obras Completas*. Madrid: Aguila, 1942–1950.

——. *The Golden Fountain Cafe (La Fontana de Oro)*. Trans. Walter Rubin. Pittsburgh: Latin American Literary Review Press, 1989.

Plant, Judith, and Christopher Plant, eds. *Putting Power in Its Place: Create Community Control!* Gabriola Island, BC: New Society Publishers, 1991.

Polsky, Milton E., *Let's Improvise: Becoming Creative, Expressive and Spontaneous Through Drama*. Englewood Cliffs, N.J.: Prentice-Hall, 1980; New York: Applause, 1997.

Proust, Marcel. *Remembrance of Things Past*. Trans. C.K. Scott Moncrieff and Terence Kilmartin. 1924. New York: Random House, 1981; Vintage, 1982.

Pure, Michel de. *La Prètieuse*. Paris: E. Droz, 1938–1939.

Quennell, Peter, ed. *Affairs of the Mind: The Salon in Europe and America from the Eighteenth to the Twentieth Century*. Washington, D.C.: New Republic Books, 1980.

Rapoport, Amos. *Human Aspects of Urban Form: Towards a Man-Environment Approach to Urban Form and Design*. New York: Pergamon, 1977.

Récamier, Jeanne Francoise Julie Adélaïde Bernard. *Memoirs and Correspondence of Madame Récamier*. Trans. and ed. Isaphene M. Luyster. 1867. New illustrated edition. New York: AMS, 1975.

Rheingold, Howard. *They Have a Word for It: A Lighthearted Lexicon of Untranslatable Words and Phrases*. Los Angeles: Tarcher, 1988.

———. *The Virtual Community: Homesteading on the Electronic Frontier*. New York: HarperPerennial, 1994.

Saal, Rollene. *The New York Public Library Guide to Reading Groups*. New York: Crown, 1995.

Sanger, Margaret. *Margaret Sanger: An Autobiography*. 1938. New York: Dover, 1971.

Schuman, Jo Miles. *Art From Many Hands: Multicultural Art Projects for Home and School*. Englewood Cliffs, N.J.: Prentice-Hall, 1981.

Shaffer, Carolyn R., and Kristin Anundsen. *Creating Community Anywhere: Finding Support and Connection in a Fragmented World*. Forward by M. Scott Peck. New York: Putnam, 1993.

Sheeran, Michael J. *Beyond Majority Rule: Voteless Decisions in the Religious Society of Friends*. Philadelphia: Philadelphia Yearly Meeting, 1983.

Shook, E. Victoria. *Ho'oponopono: Contemporary Uses of a Hawaiian Problem-Solving Process*. Honolulu: University of Hawaii Press, 1985.

Simonson, Rick, and Scott Walker, eds. *The Graywolf Annual Five: Multicultural Literacy: Opening the American Mind*. St. Paul, Minn.: Graywolf, 1988.

Slater, Philip Elliot. *A Dream Deferred: America's Discontent and the Search for a New Democratic Ideal*. Boston: Beacon Press, 1991.

Slezak, Ellen, ed. *The Book Group Book: A Thoughtful Guide to Forming and Enjoying a Stimulating Book Discussion Group*. Chicago: Chicago Review Press, 1995.

Sokolov, Raymond A. *Native Intelligence*. New York: Harper & Row, 1975.

Sommer, Robert. *Personal Space: The Behavioral Basis of Design*. Englewood Cliffs, N.J.: Prentice-Hall, 1969.

Spolin, Viola. *Improvisation for the Theater: A Handbook of Teaching and Directing Techniques*. 1963. Evanston, Ill.: Northwestern University Press, 1999.

Starhawk. *Dreaming the Dark: Magic, Sex, and Politics*. Fifteenth Anniversary Edition. Boston: Beacon, 1997.

Steffens, Lincoln. *The Autobiography of Lincoln Steffens.* 1937. New York: Harcourt, Brace & World, 1968.

Stein, Gertrude. *The Autobiography of Alice B. Toklas.* 1933. New York: Vintage, 1990.

Stein, Ruthe. "Book Clubs in the TV Age." *San Francisco Chronicle,* March 23, 1989.

———. "Don't Expect Them to Read It Your Way." *San Francisco Chronicle,* May 23, 1989.

Steinwachs, Barbara, and Sivasailam Thiagarajan. *Barnga: A Simulation Game on Cultural Clashes.* Yarmouth, Maine: Intercultural, 1990.

Stupar, Camille M. "Cafe Salons." *CUPS, a cafe journal,* November 1992.

Sylvander, Carolyn Wedin. *Jessie Redmon Fauset: Black American Writer.* Troy, N.Y.: Whitston, 1981.

Talbot, Michael. *The Holographic Universe.* New York: HarperCollins, 1991.

Tannen, Deborah. *You Just Don't Understand: Women and Men in Conversation.* New York: Morrow, 1990.

Thompson, Charles. *What a Great Idea!: Key Steps Creative People Take.* New York: HarperPerennial, 1992.

Thompson, Robert Farris. *Flash of the Spirit: African and Afro-American Art and Philosophy.* New York: Random House, 1983; Vintage, 1984.

Thurman, Wallace. *Infants of the Spring.* 1932. Boston: Northeastern University Press, 1992.

Tinker, Chauncey Brewster. *The Salon and English Letters: Chapters on the Interrelations of Literature and Society in the Age of Johnson.* 1915. New York: Gordian, 1967.

Trouncer, Margaret. *Madame Récamier.* London: MacDonald, 1949.

Van Erven, Eugène. *The Playful Revolution: Theatre and Liberation in Asia.* Bloomington: Indiana University Press, 1992.

Van Vechten, Carl. *Nigger Heaven.* 1926. Urbana: University of Illinois Press, 2000.

Vaughan, Frances E. *Awakening Intuition.* New York: Anchor/Doubleday, 1979.

Vidal, Mary. *Watteau's Painted Conversations: Art, Literature, and Talk in Seventeenth- and Eighteenth-Century France.* New Haven, Conn.: Yale University Press, 1992.

Walker, Scott, ed. *The Graywolf Annual Ten: Changing Community.* St. Paul, Minn.: Graywolf, 1993.

Watson, Steven. *Strange Bedfellows: The First American Avant-Garde.* New York: Abbeville, 1991.

Webster, T.B.L. *Athenian Culture and Society.* Berkeley: University of California Press, 1973.

Wedgwood, C.V. *Richelieu and the French Monarchy.* Revised edition. New York: Collier, 1962.

Wells, Richard Alfred. *Manners, Culture and Dress of the Best American Society: Including Social, Commercial and Legal Forms, Letter Writing, Invitations, etc.* Omaha, Nebr.: Clark, 1891.

Westley, Dick. *Good Things Happen: Experiencing Community in Small Groups.* Mystic, Conn.: Twenty-Third Publications, 1992.

Whitmyer, Claude, ed. *In the Company of Others: Making Community in the Modern World.* Forward by Eric Utne. Los Angeles: Tarcher/Perigree, 1993.

Winokur, Jon, comp. and ed. *True Confessions.* New York: Plume; Duttun, 1992.

Wintz, Cary D. *Black Culture and the Harlem Renaissance.* 1988. College Station: Texas A&M University Press, 1997.

Wurman, Richard Saul. *Information Anxiety: What to Do When Information Doesn't Tell YouWhat You Need to Know.* Revised edition. New York: Bantam, 1990.

Young, Bob. "Cashing in on Indian Spirituality." *Casco Bay Weekly,* online edition, April 1, 1993.

INDEX

Facilitator's Guide to Participatory Decision-Making

Sam Kaner, with Lenny Lind, Duane Berger,
Catherine Toldi & Sarah Fisk

Provides the tools to put democratic values into
practice in groups and organizations. Designed to
help groups increase participation and collaboration,
promote mutual understanding, honor diversity, and
make effective, inclusive, participatory decisions, it is
loaded with graphics, guidelines and hand outs, and
presents more than 200 valuable tools and skills.
It is perfect for managers, participants, seasoned
practitioners, and students of working group dynamics.

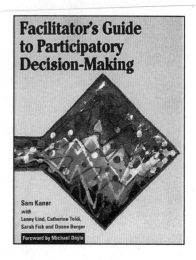

272 pages 8.5" x 11" Heavily illustrated

Hand-outs Bibliography

Pb US$26.95 / ISBN 0-86571-347-2

The Art of Focused Conversation

100 Ways to Access Group Wisdom in the Workplace

R. Brian Stanfield and the Institute for Cultural Affairs

Communication within many organizations has been
reduced to email, electronic file transfer, and hasty
sound bytes at hurried meetings. This book restores
conversation — the most human of attributes — to
prime place within businesses and organizations,
demonstrating what can be accomplished through the
medium of focused conversation. Developed, tested,
and extensively used by professionals in the field of
organizational development, it is an invaluable resource
for all working to improve communications in firms and
organizations.

240 pages 7.25" x 9"

ICA series ISBN 0-86571-416-9

Pb US$21.95 / Can $31.95

Widening Circles
A Memoir
Joanna Macy

In this absorbing memoir, well-known eco-philosopher,
Buddhist scholar, and deep ecology activist/teacher
Joanna Macy recounts her adventures of mind and spirit in
the key social movements of our era.

From involvement with the CIA and the Cold War,
through experiences in Africa, India and Tibet, to her
encounter with the Dalai Lama and Buddhism which led to
her life-long embrace of the religion and a deep commitment to the peace and environmental movements, Macy's
autobiography reads like a novel as she reflects on how her
marriage and family life enriched her service to the world.
Widening Circles reveals the unique synthesis of spirituality
and activism that define Macy's contribution to the world.

Joanna Macy is a teacher and tireless workshop leader from Berkeley, California.
(See also: *Coming Back to Life* (p.25) and *Thinking Like a Mountain* (p. 28).)

296 pages 6" x 9", PbUS$17.95 / Can$22.95 ISBN 0-86571-420-7

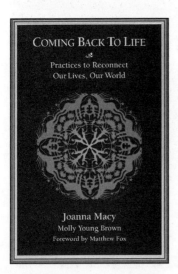

Coming Back to Life
Practices to Reconnect our Lives, Our World
Joanna R. Macy & Molly Young Brown

Many of us feel called upon to respond to the ecological
destruction of our planet, yet we feel overwhelmed
and unable to deal realistically with the threats to life on
Earth. *Coming Back to Life* provides an expansion of
Macy's pioneering work, *Despair and Personal Power in
the Nuclear Age* which, since 1983, has sold 30,000
copies. At the interface between spiritual breakthrough
and social action, *Coming Back to Life* discusses with
extraordinary insight the angst of our era, and then points
forward to the way out of apathy.

240 pages   6" x 9", ISBN 0-86571-391-X

Meditations on Everything Under the Sun
The Dance of Imagination, Intuition, and Mindfulness

Margo Adair

Foreword by Angeles Arrien

This ground-breaking work by one of the country's foremost meditation teachers is as wholistic an approach to a healthy psyche as Andrew Weil's guide is to physical health. It weaves together three consciousness disciplines and includes 160 meditations on virtually every issue people face in contemporary life; plus dozens designed for enhancing collaboration in groups. Designed for both professionals and general readers, using this book enables everyone to put their best foot forward.

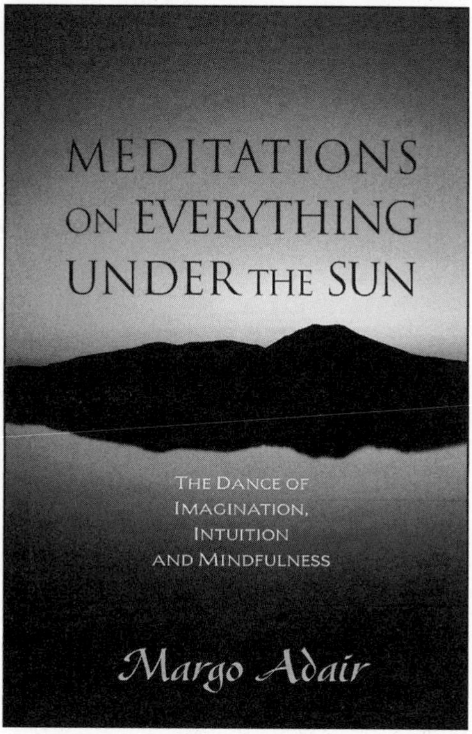

Margo Adair is the founder of Tools for Change, an organization dedicated to facilitating both personal and social transformation. Her previous book *Working Inside Out* (Wingbow Press, 1985) sold over 40,000 copies, remaining on BookPeople's top 10 bestseller list for years. Adair is interviewed on public radio programs regularly and travels extensively conducting workshops. She lives in both Seattle and San Francisco.

408 pages 6" x 9" Index

ISBN 0-86571-428-2

US$19.95 / Can$27.95

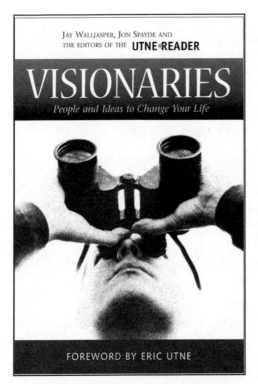

Visionaries

People and Ideas to Change Your Life

Jay Walljasper, Jon Spayde, and the Editors of UTNE READER

Foreword by Eric Utne

Praised by *The New York Times* as "one of the most distinctive voices in magazine journalism," the *Utne Reader's* mission has been to uncover the important and inspiring news that the major media overlook. Now, with that same dedication, the editors of *Utne* have profiled more than sixty of the world's most original thinkers who are often right at the center of that news, focusing on their ideas, their inspiration, and their visions of the future.

These are not the "visionaries" usually lauded in the major media who tell us how the world of tomorrow will be shaped overwhelmingly by globalization, new technology, and market economics. Coming from monasteries and urban ghettos, working at architecture firms and restaurants, living in Berkeley and Bangladesh, being under 35 and over 80, the visionaries in this book share one crucial asset: hope for the future. Hope for finding broader meaning and greater joy in our lives. Hope for the restoration of the planet. Hope for a social and economic order that uses the welfare of the weakest, not the strongest, as its gauge of success. Well-illustrated with photographs of the subjects who are grouped into six categories — spirit, design, environment, social action, health, and culture — *Visionaries* is an inspiring and invaluable resource that will have profound appeal for activists, concerned citizens and all those "cultural creatives" who make up *Utne's* 600,000 loyal readers. Featuring:

- Nobel Peace Prize winner, Thich Nhat Hahn
- Catholic priest, Thomas Berry
- Sustainable business guru, Paul Hawken
- Pagan witch, Starhawk
- Eco-architect, William McDonough
- Feminist scholar, bell hooks

304 pages 6" x 9"   ISBN 0-86571-445-2   US$17.95 / Can$23.95 — available Sept. 2001

If you have enjoyed *Salons: The Joy of Conversation,*
you might also enjoy other

BOOKS TO BUILD A NEW SOCIETY

Our books provide positive solutions for people who
want to make a difference. We specialize in:

Sustainable Living • Ecological Design and Planning
Natural Building & Appropriate Technology • New Forestry
Environment and Justice • Conscientious Commerce
Progressive Leadership • Resistance and Community • Nonviolence
Educational and Parenting Resources

For a full list of NSP's titles, please call 1-800-567-6772 or check out our web site at:
www.newsociety.com

New Society Publishers

ENVIRONMENTAL BENEFITS STATEMENT

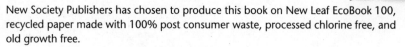

New Society Publishers has chosen to produce this book on New Leaf EcoBook 100,
recycled paper made with 100% post consumer waste, processed chlorine free, and
old growth free.

For every 5,000 books printed, New Society saves the following resources:[1]

29	Trees
2,609	Pounds of Solid Waste
2,870	Gallons of Water
3,744	Kilowatt Hours of Electricity
4,742	Pounds of Greenhouse Gases
20	Pounds of HAPs, VOCs, and AOX Combined
7	Cubic Yards of Landfill Space

---

[1]Environmental benefits are calculated based on research done by the Environmental Defense Fund and
other members of the Paper Task Force who study the environmental impacts of the paper industry.

For more information on this environmental benefits statement, or to inquire about environmentally
friendly papers, please contact New Leaf Paper – info@newleafpaper.com Tel: 888 • 989 • 5323.

NEW SOCIETY PUBLISHERS